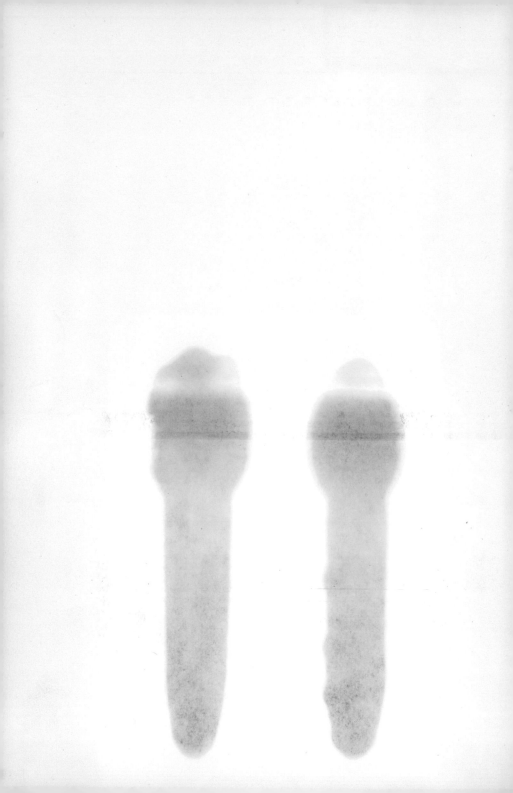

# SECOND
# SPRING

# SECOND
# SPRING:

## The Coming of Age of U.S. Catholicism

Charles A. Fracchia

**HARPER & ROW, PUBLISHERS, San Francisco**
Cambridge, Hagerstown, Philadelphia, New York,
London, Mexico City, São Paulo, Sydney

*1817*

FIRST EDITION

Designed by Design Office/Bruce Kortebein

Library of Congress Cataloging in Publication Data

Fracchia, Charles A., 1937–
  Second spring.

  Bibliography: p. 174
  1. Catholic Church in the United States—History.
  2. United States—Church history. I. Title.
  BX1406.2F72     282′.73     79-3599
  ISBN 0-06-063012-4

80 81 82 83 84 10 9 8 7 6 5 4 3 2 1

# TABLE OF CONTENTS

## DEDICATION

I dedicate this book to those who have contributed to my religious and spiritual formation:
to my parents, Charles and Josephine Fracchia
to the Sisters of the Holy Family
to the parish priests at All Souls Church in South San Francisco, California
to the Society of Jesus, particularly Edmond Smyth, S.J.; James Healy, S.J.; Robert Maloney, S.J.; William Monihan, S.J.; and R. I. Burns, S.J., with the hope that that Institute will always remain faithful to the spirit of its founder.

# ACKNOWLEDGMENTS

Any author's book is the result of many contributions; and, while the author must bear the ultimate responsibility for its views and its construction, he or she must also acknowledge those who have helped in its development. This book has benefited from numerous sources: innumerable ideas, suggestions, and discussions centering around the phenomenon of U.S. Catholicism. From each person who contributed to these pages I gathered new insights and an expanded consciousness about the Catholic Church in the United States—whether or not I agreed with their points of view.

I should acknowledge my indebtedness to Rev. Joseph Diebels, S.J.; Brother David Steindel-Rast, O.S.B.; Rev. Robert Maloney, S.J.; Tom Jordan; Rev. Thomas Splain, S.J.; Professor Eugene Bianchi; George Devine; Rev. Basil Pennington, O.C.S.O.; Professor Jacob Needleman; Theodore Roszak; Dr. Kevin Starr; and the Rev. C.M. Buckley, S.J., for their generous time in discussing with me various aspects of U.S. Catholicism.

The Gleeson Library at the University of San Francisco, with its excellent religion and theology collection, was an invaluable resource for books and periodicals. I wish to thank Paul Birkel, its librarian; and Mary Sue Cohn, Betty Scully, Ellen Carlin, Joy Moss, Bob Brethauer, Janet Underwood, Joyce Kho, and Archana Chakrabaturi, dedicated members of its staff, for their warm and generous help and attention to my needs.

To my editor, Marie Cantlon, and to Tom Dorsaneo, both of Harper & Row, I express my gratitude and appreciation for their support and suggestions during the writing of this book and in preparing it for publication.

To Sharon Moore, who typed the manuscript and also offered valuable suggestions, I offer both my gratitude and love for her unfailing support and encouragement.

CHARLES A. FRACCHIA

*Feast of the Chair of St. Peter*
*February 22, 1980*
*San Francisco*

# The World of U.S. Catholicism: A Personal Perspective

.

> *The landmines awaiting those who would write about the*
> *Catholic people today, of course, make angels fear to tread. I*
> *do not write this eagerly, but because others, who have richer*
> *tongues, are silent. Everywhere one sees disarray, confusion,*
> *division.* MICHAEL NOVAK, All the Catholic People

I am of immigrant stock. The U.S. Catholic Church is of immigrant stock. I was born in 1937. The U.S. Catholic Church has its roots in the sixteenth century in those parts of the United States that were formed from former Spanish possessions, and in the seventeenth century in the original British thirteen colonies. I was born into a world that was "different": that distinctive U.S. phenomenon, the U.S. Catholic Church.

This book is an attempt to chronicle the changes in that Church in the United States—its immigrant past, with its characteristic growth, stability, uniformity, and loyalty; the violent upheavals that marked the second half of the 1960s and the first half of the 1970s; and the trends that characterize the contemporary Church. To do this I must intrude my own perspective, or in the colloquial, describe "where I'm coming from."

At forty-three years of age, I am part of the last generation that experienced the U.S. Catholic Church as a church of immigrants, and as it functioned before the Second Vatican Council. I was born in South San Francisco, a small working-class community. My father emigrated to the United States from Monaco as a boy. He worked for the Bethlehem Steel Company in the open hearth for forty years. My mother was born in Memphis, Tennessee, of parents newly arrived from northern Italy. My parents raised three sons, of whom I was the oldest. Their frugal lives were spent in hard work; and central to their lives was Catholicism.

I responded strongly to this all-pervasive Catholicism in my family. The importance of the Church in my life permeates my earliest memories. Going to mass with my parents was a thrilling experience. Association with the parish priests at All Souls Church and with the Sisters of the Holy Family, who taught catechism in the parish before it constructed a parochial school, was always deeply satisfying. My earliest longing was to be a priest—a goal I shared with many young Catholic boys (just as many Catholic girls dreamed of becoming nuns). For most, it was an ambition that flickered out. And though I entered the Jesuit Novitiate of the Sacred Heart on August 14, 1956, I did not complete my studies for the priesthood. The parish fund-raising activities—the annual bazaar, monthly bingo games, the Buck-of-the-Month Club—involved my parents, and, as I grew older, myself. From the time I was six years of age, I was an altar boy. The Church's liturgical cycle—Christmas, Lent, Easter, Pentecost, holy days of obligation, the feast days of saints—had more meaning for me than the seasons of the year. The social life of my family centered around the church. All my family's friends were Italian Catholics. My father belonged to the Young Men's Institute and later to the Knights of Columbus; my mother was active in the Catholic Daughters of America. There were missions, novenas, and days of recollection, and of course daily mass, confession on Saturday, and other liturgical and sacramental events.

Each passage of my life was marked by the Church's active presence: shortly after I was born, I was baptized; at six years of age I went to confession and made my first communion; in early puberty I was confirmed; and, when I was married, it was with a nuptial mass.

This constant stream of events at our parish engaged a good deal of my family's time and energy, just as they engaged much of the time and energy of the entire Catholic community in South San Francisco. This socializing with friends and neighbors at All Souls Church and in parishes throughout the United States has always struck me as an important component of the appeal of U.S. Catholicism to the countless immigrants who flocked to this country.

If I was troubled about something, I would seek out one of the parish priests or one of the nuns who taught me catechism during my grammar school years to discuss whatever it was that was bothering me. This was an age before psychiatry became popular, before the human potential movement, before the plethora of self-help books and articles that became such a feature of life during the 1960s and 1970s. When I sought out a priest or nun for counseling, I was doing what virtually all Catholics did before the 1960s.

It is important to point out that my experience was duplicated in millions of households throughout the United States. I may have been somewhat more pious as a boy than some of my peers; but essentially my contemporaries, and generations of immigrant and immigrant-descended Catholics before me, grew up with the Roman Catholic Church very much in the center of their lives.

The Church's importance in my life diminished considerably after I was married. The struggle to build a career, to raise the three children who came to us at the rate of one a year, the confusion in Catholicism that began in the mid-1960s, and my life in a pluralistic society all combined to lessen my involvement in Catholicism. Grace was said at each meal, as it had been when I was growing up. My family and I went to mass each Sunday. The children had their lives marked by the same sacramental occasions as I did. But something had changed. There were no statues or holy pictures on the walls. My grandmother was no longer around to produce her splendid pastry, the same as those made traditionally in northern Italy on the Feast of St. Joseph. I no longer pored through the pages of *Liturgical Arts, Jubilee,* or *Worship.* Nor were the theology of St. Thomas Aquinas or the nature of Catholicism in the novels of Evelyn Waugh among my passionate interests or discussed among my friends any more. The changes brought about by the Second Vatican Council—particularly the liturgical changes—were unsatisfying and bewildering. I went to mass out of a sense of duty, not with the sense of community that had been a factor during my youth; and I missed the Latin Tridentine mass.

The teachings of the Church were becoming unclear and confusing. In 1965, after the birth of my third child, my wife's obstetrician warned her against any pregnancies too soon after this birth. My conscience demanded that I go to a priest for permission to use a birth control method other than the obviously ineffective rhythm method that had produced three children in three years. Although he assured me that the circumstances probably warranted the use of contraceptives and that my wife and I should follow our consciences, I always felt a bit guilty about the use of artificial birth control.

Separation, divorce, and financial collapse punctuated my life in 1970. My apathetic stance toward the Church continued during the 1970s. But, in the mid-1970s, I became more and more interested in religion—especially the phenomenon of Eastern religions which were then becoming popular in the United States. And slowly, a nagging inner voice urged me to reexamine my own religious faith—which had become such a reduced factor in my life.

The Roman Catholic Church that I examined in the 1970s was a pale shadow of its former self, a shattered institution—an institution whose collapse has been described by John Kenneth Galbraith as the greatest social displacement to occur within his lifetime. It was exhausted and vitiated from a decade of strife. It had no leadership. It no longer seemed to matter in people's lives— not as it had up to the mid-1960s.

My personal religious and spiritual odyssey, which led me eventually to pursue a doctorate in theology at the Graduate Theological Union at the University of California at Berkeley, became a dual venture. First, it was a process by which I reassessed my own relationship with the Church and focused on the nature of my faith. Second, I became fascinated with the transformation of the Church in which I had been baptized during my own lifetime. True, I had changed and grown older, but the Catholic Church of the 1970s was unarguably a very different institution than the one in which I had grown up.

Thus, while one can describe the era of disintegration of U.S. Catholicism, quote statistics on the decline in vocations and the numbers of priests, nuns, and brothers who have left their vocations, and even capture the mood of a deteriorating institution, it becomes much more difficult to ascribe precise reasons for this disintegration. The reader must realize that there is as yet no proof for anyone to declare that the change in the ecclesiastical laws concerning not eating meat on Fridays, the changes in the liturgy, or the challenges to ecclesiastical authority following the Second Vatican Council caused the mass abandonment of Catholic practices among U.S. Catholics. Nor can we say that the reason was the issuance of *Humanae Vitae*. As I propose in this book, the reasons for this deterioration are complex, not yet fully determined, and probably arise as much from the ethos of U.S. society as they do from the events which were occurring in the Catholic Church at that time.

As I struggled with the dimensions of my own spiritual life, I also examined the transformation of U.S. Catholicism. I pondered authority in the Church: for example, how could I reject its teaching on birth control while accepting other doctrines and still consider myself a practicing Catholic? By picking and choosing what I would believe, as millions of U.S. Catholics were doing in the matter of birth control, was I not denying a fundamental premise of Catholicism: its teaching authority? More and more, I began to see my religious experience in terms of a collective national Catholic experience. I also realized that those who had been born Catholic after about 1955 did not know the church that generations of U.S. Catholics had known. What would be the U.S. Catholic experience for them? How would they relate to the Catholic Church? If their religious experience in Catholicism was rooted in the Church of the post-Second Vatican Council, would their perceptions of the Church be different than those of my contemporaries and myself?

It became obvious to me that in the history of the U.S. Catholic Church the transitional period of the 1960s and 1970s was a watershed. It is difficult to account for the sudden collapse of an institution that once had commanded the unswerving loyalty of most of its members. It is difficult to understand the curtailment and cessation of prescribed religious practices by millions of U.S. Catholics within a very few years; and to assess why a once thriving institution—the cynosure of other U.S. religious denominations for its ability to receive unswerving loyalty from almost all of its members and for its ability to call upon its members to sacrifice from their meager resources to build and maintain countless institutions—suddenly became embattled.

Thus arose the concept for this book: a view of the U.S. Catholic Church that would examine the Church as it existed before the Second Vatican Council, describe the changes and tumult that occurred during and after the council, and comment on the trends visible in contemporary U.S. Catholicism. In some ways, this book is a premature exploration of these phenomena. The historian, the sociologist, the anthropologist, the psychologist still have much work to do in collecting and interpreting the data of institutional rise, decline, and transformation before a definitive study of U.S. Catholicism can be attempted. We are too close to the events of the past decade and a half to see them in perspective.

And yet, the work of description and interpretation must begin somewhere. Much of the source material for the study I undertake in this book resides in the memories and recollections of those U.S. Catholics who actively participated in the events of recent years: priests and nuns who departed from their vocations and those who remained, laypersons who fought against conciliar changes and those who labored mightily to introduce them into the U.S. Catholic Church, Catholics who left the Church and those who stayed, theologians who expounded radical change and those who espoused traditional doctrines. I have described the phenomenon of growing up Catholic from my own experiences, but these experiences were sufficiently common in the preconciliar U.S. Catholic Church to be of universal application. These diverse recollections form a substantial part of the crucible of interpretation that is the basis for this book.

Where, then, does the future direction of U.S. Catholicism lie? What will be the profile of the U.S. Catholic Church during the 1980s? To attempt to prophesy is always a dangerous task; but the trends that have become visible in U.S. Catholicism after a decade and a half of tumult and radical change give some clues to its direction and to those areas to which both the leadership and the members of the Church should address themselves. If one observes and listens carefully, the demand for a revitalization of the U.S. Catholic Church is there.

The Church fulfills best the message of salvation proclaimed by Jesus Christ to mankind when it responds to two factors: spirituality and community. The expression "people of God," used in the documents of the Second Vatican Council, resonates with both of these factors, calling to mind God's covenant with the people of Israel. And despite what is looked upon today as the naive spirituality and narrow community of the preconciliar U.S. Catholic Church, it contained both spirituality and community in abundance. The future reconstruction and renewal of the U.S. Catholic Church must recognize this rich heritage and build upon it. If, as the twelfth century humanist scholar Bernard of Chartres maintained, "We are but pygmies standing on the shoulders of giants," an understanding of what fulfilled the needs of U.S. Catholics in the years before the Second Vatican Council must be a prelude to the coming of age of the U.S. Catholic Church in the 1980s—and beyond.

This book does not attempt to provide a blueprint for the reconstruction of U.S. Catholicism. It does attempt an impressionist study of the Church before the Second Vatican Council, a description of the transitional period of the U.S. Church in the decade following the council—a period during which the U.S. Church was torn apart by dissension—an assessment of the developments which have occurred in contemporary U.S. Catholicism, and, finally, offers some suggestions for recovery from more than a decade of institutional collapse: to once again become a potent, vital spiritual force.

There is always great danger in commenting on a religious movement in terms of its tangible presence: and this danger is one of which I have been constantly aware. It is obvious that the Catholic Church cannot be assessed in terms of numbers of adherents, numbers of clergy and religious, wealth and power, churches and other institutions. It is by the spiritual life of its members that any religious body is judged—and that judgment is reserved to God. However, any church is also a visible body, an institution; and it is that institutional body which I have attempted to describe. To argue that the U.S. Catholic Church is more or less holy in 1980 than it was in 1950 is absurd. To say that it is less possible to achieve sanctity as a Catholic in 1980 than it was in 1950 is nonsense. One might speculate, however, whether the U.S. Catholic Church as an institution is healthy and effective, and whether that institution is functioning well as a vehicle for promoting the sanctity of its members and those outside of it. This concept is explored later in this book.

It is appropriate here to mention some further thoughts about my own relationship to the U.S. Catholic Church. I emphasize in this book that the Catholic Church in the United States has to be understood in terms of the hordes of Catholic immigrants who poured into the United States from the mid-nineteenth century up to the time of World War I. I believe that the principal reason for the disintegration of the U.S. Catholic Church from the mid-1960s to the mid-1970s was that the immigrant experience for the Church had ended; the assimilation of generations of the descendants of these immigrants into the mainstream of society in the United States had become an almost accomplished process.* Further, the confluence of the Second Vatican Council with the spirit of rebellion and demand for an overhauling of U.S. society that characterized this period acted in concert to produce the tumultuous events in U.S. Catholicism during the decade following the Second Vatican Council. The leadership of the U.S. Catholic Church, used to unquestioning conformity on the part of priests, religious, and laity, was unable to cope with these changes.

To lament the past—as many U.S. Catholics have done—is to deny the present and the future. This does not mean that every change that occurred after the Second Vatican Council must be condoned. For example, I welcomed liturgical reform, but excoriated the implementation of this reform. I applauded the end of the narrow authoritarianism of the Holy Office, but was shocked at the theological excesses that followed.

The point of view I express in this book studiously avoids the conservative/liberal polarity that wracked U.S. Catholicism in the decade following the Second Vatican Council; and instead is based on my assumption that the Roman Catholic Church continues to be faithful to its historic mission and that it is still *mater* and *magistra.*

I make this declaration unabashedly—despite my sometimes intense criticism in these pages of the ecclesiastical leadership in the U.S. Catholic Church, and despite my occasionally harsh critique of the effects of this inept leadership.

---

* This statement is not entirely true. New waves of immigrants, mostly of Hispanic origin, are settling in many urban areas of the United States. However, their impact on U.S. Catholicism has not been comparable to that of the Catholic immigrants of the nineteenth and early twentieth centuries.

# first spring:

THE U.S. CATHOLIC CHURCH BEFORE THE
SECOND VATICAN COUNCIL

# 1| Growing Up Catholic

*We grew up different. There were some places we went, and others did not—into the confessional box, for instance. There were also places we never went, though others could—we were told from youth to stay out of non-Catholic churches. . . . The habits of childhood are tenacious, and Catholicism was first experienced by us as a vast set of intermeshed childhood habits—prayers offered, heads ducked in unison, crossings, chants, christenings, grace at meals; beads, altar, incense, candles; nuns in the classroom alternately too sweet and too severe, priests garbed black on the street and brilliant at the altar; churches lit and darkened, clothed and stripped, to the rhythm of liturgical recurrences; the crib in winter, purple Februaries, and lilies in the spring; confession as intimidation and comfort (comfort, if nothing else, that the intimidation was survived), communion vs. revery and discomfort; faith as a creed, and creed as cathechism, Latin responses, salvation by rote, all things going in a rhythm, memorized, all things always returning, eternal in that sense, no matter how transitory.* GARRY WILLS, Bare Ruined Choirs

How central the experience of the Mass is to my life and to the lives of other U.S. Catholics. Thousands of Spanish and French missionaries had celebrated mass for hundreds of years before I was born in what is today the United States: in the swamps of Florida, in the deserts of the Southwest, in the forests of New England, and in the plains flanking the Mississippi River. In 1634, when the Calverts from England established the colony of Maryland, it was for the purpose of English Catholics being able to attend mass without the penalties that had prevailed since the mid-sixteenth century. The tiny minority of Catholics in Maryland and the other British colonies did not long enjoy this freedom, however. It was not until the end of the eighteenth century, when the enlightened founders of the United States, having successfully led a revolution against Great Britain, decided that no state religion would be established and that all citizens could worship as they pleased, that Catholics had the freedom to attend mass.

The mass was my heritage—as it was the heritage of all U.S. Catholics. I didn't mind that it hadn't changed in five centuries: in fact, this stability, this tradition, had a great deal of appeal. The mysterious ritual, conducted in a language no one but the priest understood, riveted me in hushed awe. Shivers ran down my spine at certain moments during the mass: I trembled with an almost erotic delight.

Such romantic sensibilities were not shared by everyone—although they were more common than I then realized. But only a small percentage of those who had been born Catholic in the United States would ever think of not attending mass on Sundays and holy days of obligation. Whether it was because of habit, family pressure, or fear of eternal damnation, U.S. Catholics went to mass. But habit, pressure, and fear are insufficient motivation for such extraordinary fidelity to the Church's precepts on mass-attendance. The mass was the focal point of each Catholic's sense of community in those pre-Vatican II days: and it was the primary expression of spirituality.

It was a damp South San Francisco morning in the fall of 1950. I had walked through the foggy predawn darkness from my home to All Souls Church—nearly a mile—to take my turn serving as an altar boy at the seven o'clock mass. I was thirteen years old and in the eighth grade.

At 6:30 A.M. I entered the sacristy, put on a black cassock and white surplice, lit two candles, placed the missal on the altar, and filled two cruets with wine and water and put them on a small table near the altar. By this time Father Edward Varni, assistant pastor at All Souls Church, had arrived in the sacristy, greeted me, and begun to put on over his long black cassock the vestments that had been laid out on a long table, silently reading the prayers that must be said as each garment is put on. The day was November 30, the feast of St. Andrew the Apostle, and the chasuble, stole, and maniple that Father Varni wore were red—the liturgical color of the feasts of martyrs.

Although I had seen the parish priests at All Souls Church vest countless times, I was still fascinated by the sight. The symbolism of the garments, the smell of freshly laundered, starched linen, the swift, studied motions of the priest as he donned each article all served as an awesome prelude to the coming mysteries of the mass. I yearned to do those same things someday. In fact, when I was younger, some of my friends and I "played mass" in my backyard. We would take turns pretending to be the priest, draping an old robe of my grandmother's over our shoulders and intoning what we pretended was Latin, copying as best we could the remembered ritual of the mass. I even improvised sermons—during which I would preach on the moral duty of obeying one's parents.

On his head Father Varni placed his biretta—a black, three-cornered hat with a tassle on the top—and took in his hands the chalice, the golden cup used to hold the wine that would be transformed into the Blood of Christ at mass.

Father Varni was ready, and I was excited to be participating in the forthcoming liturgical mysteries. I rang the bell outside the door leading from the sacristy to the sanctuary and preceded Father Varni to the steps that surrounded the altar. We genuflected together in front of the tabernacle: Father Varni ascended the steps, placed the chalice on the altar, opened the missal, and came back down.

Standing, while I knelt, Father Varni made the sign of the cross and began the prayers, which we intoned back and forth in Latin at the foot of the altar. "In nomine Patris, et Filii, et Spiritus Sancti. Amen. Introibo ad altare Dei." "Ad Deum qui laetificat juventutem meam," I responded. "I will go unto the altar of God. Unto God, who giveth joy to my youth."

At the conclusion of these prayers, Father Varni climbed the three steps to the altar, kissed the altar stone (which contained the relics of martyrs), moved to the "Epistle side"—the extreme right-hand side of the altar as you face it—and, with his back to me and the approximately fifty people in the church, proceeded with the mass: reading in Latin the introit, the collect, the epistle, and the gradual. As he began the gradual, he placed his left hand momentarily on the altar. This was the signal for me to stand up, genuflect, go to the Epistle side of the altar, wait for Father Varni to finish the gradual, and move the missal from one side of the altar to the other. I picked up the missal and its stand, bowed toward the tabernacle, walked diagonally down the stairs, genuflected, and walked diagonally up the other side to place the missal on the Gospel side of the altar. This procedure made me somewhat nervous, since there was always the possibility of missing a step or getting my feet entangled in the hem of my cassock. I remembered once watching in horror as an altar boy who got his foot caught in this way plunged headlong down the steps. His discomfiture—and the clang of the missal stand—were always in my mind.

My careful pouring of the wine and water and the washing of the fingers during the Offertory typified my concern for a "perfect" performance of the ritual required of me. I walked slowly and precisely up and down the stairs of the altar without having to lift the hem of my cassock. My bows toward the tabernacle and the crucifix were profound. Crisp military precision, tempered with ecclesiastical languor and solemnity, were the standards for my service. After all, not only did God reside in the tabernacle; the mysterious drama of bringing Him forth from bread and wine would soon unfold: and I was a participant in this event.

Midway through the canon came the consecration. As often as I had experienced the consecration at mass, it still gave me goose bumps. It was the Last Supper reproduced there in All Souls Church. It was the actual changing of the bread and wine on the altar into the Body and Blood of Jesus Christ. It was Christ's crucifixion renewed sacramentally, but without the shedding of blood. Father Varni bowed low over the large white wafer he held in his hands. "Hoc est enim Corpus meum," he stage-whispered slowly and distinctly. He genuflected, and I rang the bell. He held the now-consecrated Host high over his head, and I rang the bell again. He genuflected, and for the third time I rang the bell.

The process was repeated with the chalice holding the wine. "Hic est enim Calix Sanguinis mei, novi et aeterni testamenti: mysterium fidei: qui pro vobis et pro multis effundetur in remissionem peccatorum," the bowed Father Varni enunciated.

The canon continued: prayers for the dead, an appeal that we might all someday join the saints in heaven, and a short prayer that we all unite ourselves to Christ.

It was time then to prepare for Communion. Father Varni recited the "Our Father" and broke the large Host in two, detaching a further small piece to put into the chalice. "Agnus Dei, qui tollis peccata mundi: miserere nobis," he said out loud. "Lamb of God, who takes away the sins of the world, have mercy on us." Priest and congregation struck their breasts.

At this point I pulled a long cloth all the way over the Communion railing that separated the sanctuary from the rest of the church. I returned to my place at the foot of the altar, reached to pick up the paten, and then accompanied Father Varni to the Communion railing. He was holding a ciborium (a large gold cup containing consecrated Hosts) that he had taken from the tabernacle. Those who were going to receive Communion were already kneeling at the railing. Several of the communicants were friends of my parents or grandparents: Mrs. Baldini, Mrs. Giustetto, Mrs. Penna. And Mr. Thompson, a black man who lived near us and whose daughter was a classmate of my brother's, was there—as he was every morning. Another friend and neighbor, Mrs. Malone, whose son Billy is one of my closest friends and a classmate, was also at the railing.

I put the paten under Mrs. Penna's chin, pushing back the knot of her black woolen kerchief. Father Varni fished out a Host and placed it on the tip of her tongue, saying, "Corpus Domini nostri Jesu Christi custodiat animam tuam in vitam aeternam. Amen." "May the Body of our Lord Jesus Christ preserve thy soul to life everlasting. Amen."

We went down the line of communicants, each of whom swallowed the Host, remained kneeling briefly, and then returned to his or her pew, kneeling there for a few moments with head bowed. After the last one received Communion, we returned to the altar. I knelt and received Communion: the small, crisp white wafer went down my throat with some difficulty. But this tasteless wafer was the Body and Blood of the Son of God; and my receiving Communion was the high moment of the experience at mass. God was within me! The sense of both awe and love I felt made me tingle with excitement.

After consuming the contents of the chalice, Father Varni said the remaining prayers of the mass and recited the last Gospel, the beautiful beginning of the Gospel of St. John. "In principio erat Verbum, et Verbum erat apud Deum, et Deus erat Verbum. . . ." When he finished, I responded, "Deo gratias," and the mass was over. Father Varni descended the steps, holding the covered chalice, and we both knelt to say the prayers after mass—for the conversion of Russia from Communist atheism. We rose; I handed Father Varni his biretta; and we walked into the sacristy.

But my duties were not yet concluded. I helped Father Varni take off his vestments, extinguished the candles on the altar, and put the cruets away.

My mother's role in my religious life was significant. I noticed her pride when I served mass. She was very pleased that I wanted to be a priest; but she would not let me go to the seminary after the eighth grade. She thought that was too young. I put a great deal of pressure on her, but she would not budge.

For as long as I can remember, my mother took me to Sunday mass and answered my questions about what was going on. Each morning when she woke me up, she knelt down next to my bed and taught me my prayers: the "Our Father," the "Hail Mary," and the "Glory be to the Father . . . " Each evening we would do the same thing, adding a prayer to my guardian angel, "Angel of God, my guardian dear, to whom God's love commits me here, be ever this day at my side . . . "

Yes, my mother was indeed a pious woman; but she was no match for some of my grandmother's friends, several of whom practically lived in church, wrapped in black shawls, lighting candles, muttering prayers *sotto voce* in Italian. Some of these women were widows; others were married to husbands who beat them, or so went the gossip. Their husbands usually committed an even greater fault in these women's eyes, however: they didn't go to church.

It was a Wednesday, and after school I rushed to All Souls Church once again. Because I went to a public grammar school, I had since kindergarten to attend two hours of religious instruction after school on Wednesday afternoons and two hours on Saturday mornings.

Those early years of catechism were exciting as I prepared to make my First Holy Communion. For months the nuns drilled me in the *Baltimore Catechism:* "Who made me?" and the answer, "God made me." "Why did God make me?" and the answer, "God made me to serve, honor and obey Him." And on it went—question after question, page after page, book after book.

I made my First Holy Communion on Mother's Day, when I was in the first grade. As that day approached, I was in a fever of anticipation. My fellow communicants-to-be and I marched and practiced under the watchful eye of Sister Joanna until she was certain that we would perform at the upcoming mass with the precision of a company of Marines.

On the day before my First Holy Communion, I was to receive another sacrament for the first time: that of penance (or "going to confession," as it was called). I can still remember the jokes my friends and I told each other nervously about what sins we were going to confess, what penance the priest would impose on us, and so forth. I stood in line outside of the confessional, silently saying again the formula of confession and reciting my sins. After what seemed to be a very long wait, with thumping heart and shaking knees I entered the small, dark box. Three small cubicles comprised the confessional. The center cubicle, which was where the priest sat, had a light that could be switched on when he wasn't hearing confession. The two cubicles flanking this one had no chairs: one could only kneel, facing the grate which opened onto the priest's cubicle.

I knelt in the tiny, blackened space, separated from the cool, quiet church by a thick curtain. The air was stuffy: I felt entombed. The priest was engaged with the penitent on the other side. I could hear whispered mumbling, but I couldn't under-

stand what was being said. Then, silence . . . and the sliding
sound of the panel being closed between the priest and the person who had been to confession . . . a rustling, and the sound of
the panel being opened to where I was waiting, kneeling in a
benumbed state.

"Yes."

"Bless me, Father, for I have sinned," I gulped. "This is my
first confession." My throat was dry, and I struggled to remember my sins.

I told Father Egan, then the assistant pastor at All Souls
Church, that I had disobeyed my parents, had hit my brother Eugene, and had lied to my teacher, Mrs. Morrison. He asked me if
I were sorry for my sins, and after I told him I was, he assigned
me a penance of one "Our Father" and one "Hail Mary." I concluded with an "Act of Contrition."

Kneeling in that dark cubicle, confessing in hushed, whispered tones to Father Egan, whom I couldn't see in the pitch
black, gave me a feeling of God's awesome power. How wonderful God was that He would forgive me my sins—no matter how
many times I had committed those sins.

Although we weren't supposed to tell anyone the sins we had
confessed, Bob Brusa, a friend of mine, did tell me that Father
Egan had corrected him when Bob told him that he had committed adultery. Bob had thought that adultery was disobeying
adults.

All day that Saturday before Mother's Day, my household had
bustled with activity. My parents had invited about fifty friends
and relatives to our home for midday dinner; and my mother
and grandmother spent the day cooking while my father bor-
rowed tables and chairs. That evening my mother taped the noz-
zles of the kitchen and bathroom sinks lest I should wake up in
my sleep and unwittingly get a glass of water: no food or drink
was allowed from midnight on the night before anyone went to
Communion.

How exciting that Mother's Day was. I was ever so careful that
not a drop of liquid should pass my lips after I had gotten up
that morning. I dressed myself in my new blue suit, and put a
white ribbon on my arm to signify purity. The anticipation of re-

ceiving Our Lord in the Eucharist was such that I was impatient to be off to church long before my family and I were scheduled to depart. Boys and girls marched into the church—boys in blue suits, girls in white dresses and veils—and passed between the pews filled with proud families and friends. Each of us had a prayer book between our folded hands. We knelt in the front pews of the church and waited breathlessly for "the big moment."

When the time came to receive Communion, I felt that invisible angels were watching me. I was going to have Jesus Christ enter me in the form of a thin white wafer of bread. This ecstatic thought was coupled with a more practical one: concern that I swallow the Host without touching it with my teeth and before it melted in my mouth. I knelt at the altar railing. The priest stood in front of me. I opened my mouth . . . and into it was placed the Body and Blood of Christ. I successfully swallowed it.

"Go, the mass is over," intoned Father Egan. First communicants and families left the church. All had gone well. Sister Joanna was proud and smiling.

Pictures were taken in front of the church and in a portrait studio. My picture—with angels in the background—is still displayed on my mother's night table. The party at my home was a big success: everyone told me how nice I looked and what a big day this was for me. And there were a great many presents.

The nine o'clock mass on Sunday was the family mass; and it was to this mass that my family and I, when I was not serving mass, went every week. First, the grammar school children would file in by class, genuflect in unison on a signal from Sister Mary Victoria's wooden clacker, and fill the pews in the front section of the church. An eighth grader, I sat with my parents and felt very grown up as I watched my brothers walk up the center aisle of the church.

It was not my turn to serve mass that Sunday, so I sat with my grandmother and parents, reading the mass in English from my daily missal as Father Varni said it in Latin. After the Gospel of the day was said in Latin, Father Varni read it in English, made a number of announcements concerning parish affairs, and delivered the sermon. In keeping with the novena to Our Lady of Lourdes in progress at All Souls Church, he spoke about the Blessed Virgin Mary as a model for Catholics.

Out of the corner of my eye I glimpsed my grandmother, muttering her rosary in nearly audible Italian; and in front of a side altar dedicated to St. Joseph, ablaze with more than a hundred lighted candles, I saw Mrs. Maladetto, a friend of my grandmother's, lighting yet another candle and placing it in front of the statue of St. Joseph.

The mass continued after Father Varni's sermon. The Offertory . . . the canon . . . the consecration, during which hundreds of heads bowed and hundreds of hands struck breasts while the altar boy jangled the bells . . . Communion . . . and then mass ended.

The parishioners of All Souls poured out into the bright sunlight. As those who were early for the ten o'clock mass began to enter the church, knots of those who had just attended mass gathered for conversation. My parents talked with our neighbors, the Canaveros, while my brothers and I chatted with some of our classmates. The Malones waved as they walked toward their car in the parking lot.

I was always amused by the socializing after mass at All Souls Church. The parish was composed of both Irish and Italians. Both groups were involved in parish work, lived next door to each other in the same neighborhoods, shopped together in the same stores. And yet it seemed that, with few exceptions, the Italian-American parishioners socialized with other Italian-Americans, and Irish-Americans with other Irish-Americans.

Although my parents' friends consisted almost entirely of other Italian families, this had become somewhat less a factor with my brothers and myself. And those of my parents' generation still urged their children to marry girls from Italian families. While dating of Catholic boys and girls was the general rule, most Italian-American parents preferred it if these Catholic boys and girls were Italian-Catholics. "Who's going to cook you gnocchi, ravioli, and all the other dishes that you like?" Bob Canavero's mother had once asked him—only half-humorously.

For my parents, the question "Is he (or she) a Catholic?" was a frequent one. It was asked about persons they met, about my friends and my brothers' friends, people they read about in the newspapers. "Is he or she one of us?" was what they really meant. My parents were cordial to non-Catholic neighbors and individuals they met; but I never knew them to have as friends any persons who were not Catholic.

A perfect example of this questioning of non-Catholics had occurred one evening when I had dinner at my friend Paul's house. His brother, Bob, was dating a Methodist girl form the local public high school. His parents hadn't said anything to him. Bob continued to date her. But their disapproval was obvious: they had mentioned the situation to my parents. The evening I was there for dinner his mother asked him point-blank, "Why are you dating Mary Ann? Can't you find any nice Catholic girls to date?"

"What's wrong with Mary Ann?" Bob asked. "She's a nice girl."

Bob's mother probably thought that all non-Catholic girls were immoral, but confined herself to quoting the pastor at All Souls.

"Do you remember what Monsignor Tozzi said about mixed marriages? He said that it was the biggest single cause of Catholics losing the faith. And he said that in order to avoid marrying a non-Catholic, Catholics should only date other Catholics."

"But, Mom," Bob replied somewhat defensively, "I'm not going to marry her. I'm just taking her out."

"Well, that's how it starts," his mother countered. "You date a non-Catholic, she wants to get married, and pretty soon you find you're married. With all the lovely Catholic girls in this city, you'd think you could find someone of your own religion to date."

The conversation ended—and so did Bob's dating of Mary Ann.

The ten o'clock mass was about to begin, and the gatherings in front of the All Souls Church began to dissolve—those who lived nearby walking to their homes, others going to their automobiles.

"How come you no serve mass today, Charlie?" I saw Mrs. Maladetto approaching, dressed in severe black and clutching her purse with both hands.

"It wasn't my turn today, Mrs. Maladetto," I replied with a smile.

She opened her handbag, squeezed open her change purse, and handed me a quarter. "Here," she announced, "buy some ice cream. When you go to the *seminario* I give you *dieci scudi*. You such a nice boy, Charlie." She always pronounced my name as if it had no "r."

I thanked her, and put the quarter in my pocket. I had learned not to refuse the old woman her occasional gifts to me.

"Charlie, let's go." It was my father calling. I said goodbye to Mrs. Maladetto, and joined my family for our ride home. In a few moments my mother would be preparing her traditional large Sunday morning breakfast while my father, brothers, and I would be reading the Sunday newspaper. I always liked Sundays.

I thought about my First Holy Communion as I entered the parish hall adjacent to the church to attend catechism class. That spring of 1950 I would receive yet another sacrament: confirmation. Sister Mary Victoria was preparing me and others of my age to become "soldiers of Christ"—which we were told was the meaning of confirmation.

When class began, Sister Mary Victoria announced that she was going to talk about purity. My interest was instantly aroused, for I knew that a discussion of purity meant a discussion of sex. In the last two or three years I had become interested in sex—not that I knew much about it. At a party this year, my classmates and I played "post office"—I kissed Paula Colvin, whom I'd had a crush on since fifth grade. I felt very confused and embarrassed, but I enjoyed it.

I also noticed that my penis often got stiff—something it hadn't done before—and that I woke up at night when I felt a sticky substance around my groin. At first I thought I was urinating, but after a few times I realized that this was something different. I finally, with great reluctance, asked my mother about it, and she told me that I had been having something called "wet dreams," which all boys experience when they are adolescents.

This explanation reassured me that nothing abnormal was happening to me. But my parents never said much more about sex to me. They were not prudish, but they never discussed sex. Occasionally, I would go barging into my mother's bedroom when she was dressing or undressing, and would see her nude. She never seemed to mind this, and I was never embarrassed by it. And I usually walked without any clothes from the bathroom to my bedroom after I had bathed or showered, parading before whoever happened to be walking by. Nobody seemed to mind except for my grandmother, who lived with us. She told me that the devil would cut off my penis at night if I walked around without any clothes. But she was smiling when she said it.

When I was in the seventh grade, my mother came up to me one day with a stack of pamphlets written by Father Daniel Lord, S.J. "Why don't you take these and read them," she announced. "You're old enough to know about sex." That may have been true, but the pamphlets didn't help much to broaden my knowledge. Telling adolescents that their bodies are "pure" and "temples of the Holy Ghost" didn't say much about tumultuously changing bodies and roller-coaster feelings; and discussion of sex in very vague terms made it all the more mysterious. And the manuals certainly didn't contain much technical information.

Sister Mary Victoria told the class that she was going to make some general comments about purity, and then she would discuss this subject separately with the girls. She began, like Father Lord, telling us that our bodies were temples of the Holy Ghost, and that they should remain pure and unsullied until marriage. (Does marriage make them impure and sullied, I wondered?) Sex, she announced, was intended by God only for those who were married. In marriage, sex was wonderful. It showed the love of men and women and it produced whatever children God wished to send. But, outside of marriage, sex was wrong and loathsome. These were "sins of the flesh." It was "lust." And this last word Sister Mary Victoria spat out with decided venom.

Everyone was listening intently. Sister Mary Victoria continued to address the class, admonishing each of us to keep away from "occasions of sin"—those circumstances which might lead to temptation overcoming our resistance to sin. Don't read "dirty" books or magazines, she told us. Don't think "dirty" thoughts or tell "dirty" jokes. And don't "neck" or "pet."

I am still embarrassed today when I remember that, at that time, I was unsure what "necking" and "petting" meant. My knowledge of sex and the reproductive system was vague and uncertain—like an ancient cosmographer's knowledge of the world. I strained my ears during that class with Sister Mary Victoria, hoping she would utter some key word that would illuminate the darkness of my knowledge of sex. But no such illumination came.

Sister Mary Victoria elaborated on the evils she had just mentioned—particularly "necking and petting." These were "illicit caresses," she said. But, if this were not enough, "necking and petting" could lead to "intimate physical contact" because they aroused our appetites; and "intimate physical contact"—sex, in other words, outside of marriage—was a mortal sin.

There was a rustling in the room: the boys and girls were standing up. Father Varni had entered the rear of the classroom. Sister Mary Victoria concluded her remarks, and asked the girls in the class to accompany her to another room. Father Varni was going to talk to the boys about purity.

He began by encouraging us not to lead girls into temptation against purity. They are trying to imitate the purity of the Blessed Virgin Mary, he said, and no boy should in any way attempt to lead astray any girl from the path of purity.

There was a pause. "Now, boys, there is something else I want to discuss with you," Father Varni said. "Sister has already mentioned to you about boys and girls not caressing each other. I want to talk to you about not touching yourselves—or masturbation, as it is sometimes called."

It soon became clear that masturbation was not about scratching your forehead, but about touching your genitals, or "private parts," as Father Varni put it. (In the adjoining room, the girls, as I learned later, were being told not to touch "down there.")

Masturbation, Father Varni warned us, was a sin. It could be a mortal sin. It could lead one into many sins of the flesh. And not only was masturbation against the law of God and that of the Church, it was also against the law of nature. God punished this sin not only in the afterlife, but here on earth as well. It was a well-known fact, said Father Varni, that those who habitually masturbated often went mad. Other could catch loathsome diseases or get warts on their hands.

Father Varni finished his talk by urging the boys to imitate the purity of Jesus Christ and His Blessed Mother, not to say, think, or do anything that one would be ashamed to say, think, or do in front of one's own mother, and to read the pamphlets, available in the vestibule of the church, written by Father Lord on purity. These were written for teenagers, said Father Varni, and they would answer any questions about sex that we might have.

I hurried because I had my newspaper route to deliver before dinner. As I walked, I thought about the talks given by Sister Mary Victoria and Father Varni—and of Judy Oliva's recapitulation of Sister's separate talk to the girls. It was all somewhat confusing and bewildering. Father Varni's comments on masturbation had made a great impact,[1] and so had Sister Mary Victoria's remarks on purity.

My childhood love of the Church grew throughout my adolescence. Its teachings struck me as sound and coherent. Its sense of community nurtured my desire to serve the religious needs of this Catholic people of God. I retained my desire to become a priest; and opted to become a Jesuit.

# 2/ Remembrances of Things Past

The millions of Catholic European immigrants who poured into the United States during the nineteenth and twentieth centuries did more than provide labor for the explosive industrial expansion of the United States, change the political complexion of the country, and introduce exotic customs into a formerly homogenous society: they gathered in their national diversity to create one of the most monolithic religious experiences of history and they forged an experiment in community and spirituality that continues to influence the lives of many who grew up in the preconciliar U.S. Catholic Church.

These influences sent by no means all Catholic young men and women into seminaries, novitiates, and convents. Although most Catholic boys and girls at some point contemplated making such a commitment, only a miniscule percentage ever actually took the solemn step of doing so; and only a minority of those ever completed the intention to ordination or vows. But that thousands each year did so said *something* about the many immigrant U.S. Catholic parents—and descendants of those immigrants—who saw their children commit themselves to lives as priests, brothers, and nuns.

Each of us was the product of the tension and the ambivalence of the U.S. Catholic experience—that of being sons of immigrant newcomers in a hostile, pagan United States. Andrew Greeley captures the essence of this experience when he writes:

The overwhelming fact about American Catholicism is that like all other Christian religious in the United States, it is a religion of immigrants. However, the Catholic immigration reached its flood tide after the establishment of the American republic as a basically Anglo-Saxon Protestant society. Thus, Catholicism was not only an immigrant religion but an immigrant religion coming into a culture which, for a number of historical reasons, was antipathetic to Catholicism. Therefore, this particular immigrant religion was faced with the dilemma of becoming American enough to survive in the new society and remaining Catholic enough to maintain its allegiance to the worldwide Roman Catholic faith.[1]

This is the basic theme of the history of Catholicism in the United States: its ambivalence about the society of which it has become a part. It is this ambivalence which was a factor in my growing up Catholic—as well as those of my confreres at the Novitiate of the Sacred Heart—an ambivalence that was shared by most U.S. Catholics for more than a century.

One viewpoint, which dates all the way back to John Carroll, the first U.S. bishop, argues that far from having to fear American society and American culture, the Catholic Church ought rather to rejoice in it, because American institutions provide an environment in which Catholicism can grow and flourish as it has nowhere else in the world. From this point of view, there are no dangers in dialogue with American democracy, but only opportunity.

The opposite viewpoint is much less sanguine about the society and culture of the United States. It is conscious that Catholicism is a minority group in a country unfriendly to it. It is aware of the strength of non-Catholic religious bigotry and the threat to the faith of Catholics, particularly Catholic immigrants, in this society. According to this viewpoint, Catholicism must be viewed as a subculture having values which are distinctly different from the values of the larger society, and it must be wary of permitting its values to be corrupted by the materialism and secularism of the society in which it finds itself.

The second viewpoint was the dominant one in U.S. Catholicism from the second quarter of the nineteenth century until the

1960s. It was this viewpoint that gave me and my fellow Jesuit novices a sense of urgency and importance about our vocations: we had been selected by God to act as the protectors of the community of U.S. Catholics.

It was a hot Friday afternoon in 1957—Good Friday, to be exact. It was a day of complete silence. A few of us Jesuit novices were cutting the grass in a field above the Sacred Heart Novitiate in Los Gatos, California. By some fluke my companions, whom I had known since high school, were among the very few novices I knew before we entered the Jesuit novitiate last year. Brother Peter M. Finnegan, Brother Frank Damrell, Brother Edmund G. Brown, Jr. (future governor of California), and I toiled with our hoes, desiring to converse but not daring to do so.

The music from *High Society*, the last movie I had seen before entering the novitiate, floated through my head, alternating with the sensual sounds of the music from *Picnic*. I felt vaguely disconcerted: images of Grace Kelly and Kim Novak kept drifting through my imagination. I strenuously attempted to banish them; but they continued to haunt me, to mock my attempts to exorcise them. Jesuits, after all, are not supposed to be disturbed by erotic visions.

That day—coincidentally during the Three Hours on Good Friday (the time from noon to 3 P.M. that commemorates the passion and death of Jesus on the Cross)—was one of the only black periods I had spent in the Jesuit novitiate. True, most of my friends would have thought the life too spare, too austere. It was not only the rigors of the life itself: up at 5 A.M., dress, an hour for meditation, mass, breakfast, manual work, class, examination of conscience, lunch, recreation, reading, work or class, reading of the *Imitation of Christ*, supper, recreation (conversation only in Latin), spiritual talk by the master of novices, benediction and litanies, to bed (a schedule varied only on Thursdays, which was "villa day," a sort of play-day, and on Sundays); it was that what most people considered important—money, fame, power, women, individual friendships—was forbidden us.

No matter, on August 14, 1956, some thirty-eight of us, from widely diverse Catholic backgrounds, had chosen this life. For nearly a year we had lived happily with the prohibitions, with the challenges, with the deprivations. All of us thought of ourselves as most fortunate. We had no keys, no money, no girlfriends; but we had the conviction that we were following a personal call from God: what we called a "vocation." And we knew, deep inside ourselves, that if we followed that call, no matter where it took us, God would reward us—not as the world would reward us, but after our earthly lives had come to an end, in heaven.

What can be said about men and women who live their lives in such a manner? That they are fools? That some youthful impulse has abstracted them from their reason, from the sources of that life that most men and women find coherent and sustaining? Perhaps: but I found that that call from God was the true culmination of my growing up Catholic in the United States.

Peter Finnegan, Jerry Brown, Frank Damrell, and I had gone to different high schools, and all of us had actively participated in our schools' debate teams. Peter had entered the novitiate after high school; the rest of us had gone first to one year of a Jesuit college. All four of us had dated during high school: and our memories of the Catholic girls we had known would linger with us during our years at Los Gatos. But those memories, no matter how distracting to us then, would not deflect us from what we felt was the *summum bonum*, "the highest good," the special call from God.

For some of us, certainly for Peter and myself, this call found a fertile, nurturing field in the piety of our families; for others, Jerry certainly, their families were somewhat hostile to this vocation. In his case, and in the cases of others, additional factors were perhaps operative. In virtually all instances, however, vocations came from the immigrant Catholic influences that shaped our lives.

In retrospect, of course, we are less idealistic about the motives for our vocations. We are more prone today to see these "calls" as outbursts of religious romanticism, channeled during the 1960s into such idealistic ventures as the Peace Corps; as an aspect of upward social mobility for immigrant Catholic families. ("You got the *lingua* [an Italian word which means *tongue:* used to indicate verbal skills]," my grandmother used to say to me. "You should become a priest or an attorney." And, indeed, an unusually large number of Catholic young men gravitated to these two careers.)

But in 1957, I felt I had been called upon by God for a life devoted exclusively to Him. That call sustained me as I crouched in the hot sun on the side of a hill, cutting grapes off the vine for the novitiate's winery, until my body was stiffened in pain. That call upheld me through a *defectus caritatis,* when I knelt for an hour in the midst of a large room, in front of the master of novices, and heard each of my fellow novices relate my faults. (I have often marveled how this feature of preconciliar religious life has been harshly criticized, while similar processes arising out of humanistic psychology, such as encounter groups at Esalen, have been more mildly treated.) And it sustained me when I was assigned disagreeable work tasks, such as killing and cleaning chickens or cleaning the "traps" in the showers.

To every seminarian and religious, the vocation was paramount. Did a young woman about to make her vows as a nun flinch when her hair was cut to within a few centimeters of her skull and forever more covered with a veil or headdress? If she did, she felt that it was a small price to pay for this wonderful gift from God—her vocation. Did a seminarian, studying for the diocesan clergy, become lonely when he returned home for summer vacation and saw his friends dating? If he did, he, too, realized that this was his state of life: he hadn't chosen it, God had chosen him. Did a teaching brother resent it when his superior assigned him to teach mathematics, when his great love was history? Well, he knew that the superior's will was God's will, and it was God's will that he must follow, not his own.

It was God's will that on Good Friday, 1957, Brother Finnegan, Brother Brown, Brother Damrell, and I hoed the grassy field in the hot sun in silence at the Novitiate of the Sacred Heart.

This vocation, this path, if persisted in, would lead to ordination to the priesthood or final vows as a religious. As such, it would give vast power to the priest or religious. The priest said mass, baptized, officiated at weddings, heard confessions, anointed the dying, conducted funerals. He was a community leader, an ombudsman, consulted by his flock on all matters of secular affairs. The duties of many priests went beyond the sacramental: they taught, were chaplains in prisons, hospitals, and for the armed forces. The bulk of religious—both men and women—taught the millions of Catholics in Catholic schools (and even those in public schools), staffed hospitals and orphanages, and performed a myriad of other tasks.

Such power was not unique to U.S. Catholicism—not even to Catholicism—but it was distinctive to the preconciliar U.S. Catholic Church. We must remember that sixty-five to seventy-five percent of U.S. Catholics—from forty to fifty million—attended weekly mass before the late 1960s. And we must keep in mind the deep loyalty, perhaps even dependence, that these millions of Catholics had to the Church and to the priests and religious of the Church. Much of it arose from the harshness of immigrant life, and much of it from the sheer fascination with men and women who had "forsaken all for Christ."

There was no comparable experience in Protestant denominations or in U.S. Judaism—despite similarities of ministry. Ministers and rabbis married and had children; they led lives not too dissimilar from those in their congregations. Neither Protestant groups nor Judaism had that most romantic embodiment of religious life—the nun. Nuns divested themselves of all the symbols of womanly fulfillment: not marrying or having children; not adorning themselves—in fact, shaving their heads and wearing the most unfashionable garb; not having friends; and not being able to venture out of the convent enclosure alone. These were the heroines of Catholicism; and their imprint on preconciliar Catholicism is incalculable.

The nuns, even more than priests or male religious, radiated chastity. A Catholic woman who bore several children, ran a household, frugally budgeted her husband's modest income, worried about having more children, and piously fulfilled her religious duties looked to nuns as superior human beings, as somehow superior religious individuals. And so did men. Most

Catholic men had been taught by nuns; and it was probably the sexual innocence of nuns that caused us to place them in a pantheon, along with our mothers, and gave them such an important place in our memories and imaginations.

Chastity. Has there been a more all-encompassing feature historically in Christianity, particularly in Catholicism? What was the genesis of this preoccupation with sexual purity, with the begrudging acceptance of even marital sexuality, with the overwhelming attention that sex has received in Christianity?

One sees little such preoccupation in the Gospels. But it is not long after Jesus Christ's life on earth that such a dualism emerges: in the writings of Paul and in those of the Church Fathers. After that it is strongly imprinted in the Christian consciousness.

What most disturbed me on that Good Friday of 1957? It was not my aching back and stiff fingers. It was not the discomfort from the hot sun. Nor was it my inability to talk with my companions—favored ones among my fellow novices, despite the prohibition against "particular relationships." No, it was my tussling with the vaguely erotic images that flitted through my mind, accompanied by the music from *High Society* and *Picnic*. And it raised a disturbing specter within me: a disconcerting sense of loneliness, an upsetting lack of tranquility.

Sex, relationships with girls and women, had always been a difficult area for me. Some of this difficulty was due to my poor self-image and the knowledge at an early age that I was "destined for God's service"; some of it was rooted in the strong impact the Church's teaching on sexuality—whether official or not—had made on me. Certainly, the fact that the U.S. Catholic Church was most strongly influenced by an Irish-based concept of sexuality, through the medium of a predominant Irish-American hierarchy and clergy, was in large part responsible for what has come to be labeled "puritanical" sexuality. But there had to be more to it than that, since I was relatively untouched by Irish-American clerics. This puritanical concept of sex influenced me as it influenced all those who grew up Catholic in the Untied States: it was in the very air of U.S. Catholicism and seeped from every pore of the Church.

Ever since the third grade, when I had noticed that I felt a special attraction for Joyce Wallin, a classmate, sex (even though I probably had not even heard the word at that time) had been one of my major preoccupations. One can counter that this is probably true of any human being; but it was different with me—as it was different with almost all U.S. Catholics.

In the fifth grade the object of my affections became Paula Colvin, another classmate, who had just moved to town. My longing for her during that period of pubescence remains deeply imprinted in my mind to this day. We never dated, however, and I only kissed her once—at a party during which post-office had been played. And, after that kiss, I wondered if I had committed a sin.

One could say that such a pious kid, who wants to be a priest, is going to have absurd scruples. And indeed, there is a certain amount of truth to that. But when I attended high school and began to date at the beginning of my junior year, I quickly discovered that I was not alone in my concepts. "Scoring" for most Catholic boys and girls in high school consisted of "making out," or "necking." Those sections of religion classes concerned with what was called "purity" aroused the most interest in students. And the annual religious retreat at each school—whether boys' or girls' high school—became dominated by sophisticated questions of moral casuistry. How long could you kiss without it being a mortal sin? asked Liz Raney at Notre Dame High School in Belmont. Is French kissing a sin? asked my classmate Jim Jackson. If your tongue touches the tongue of the boy you are kissing, is that a sin? inquired Ann Riley of the Convent of the Sacred Heart in Menlo Park. How far does your tongue have to be inserted into a boy's mouth (or vice versa) before it's a sin? wondered Sue Wallace of Mercy High School in San Mateo.

"Petting," or the touching of such parts of the body as a girl's breasts, was a more delicate subject. (The touching of a boy's genitals was beyond the pale of questioning: everybody knew that if you did this and died immediately thereafter you would go to hell.) Distinctions here multiplied. Was it OK to feel a girl's breasts if she had a sweater on? How about just a blouse? Only a brassiere? No one seemed to ask about touching a girl's bare breasts: we knew that was a sin. We might do it; but we knew we had to confess doing so.

Because the topic of sex was relegated to priests—many of whom had begun their seminary training after the eighth grade—it was they who had to field such questions, to provide sexual guidance to millions of Catholic teenagers regarding their demanding bodies, their confused feelings, and their everlasting questions. And these priests were judged by students as to how specific they were in their discussion of sex. (This basis of judgment was probably as much rooted in the delight of discussing sex as it was in moral guidance.) The priest who was vague and dogmatic was labeled boring and out of touch. But the priest who frankly discussed sexual questions was hailed as a hero—no matter what he counseled.

A host of terms and distinctions arose from these discussions: "petting above the waist" as distinguished from "petting below the waist," "kissing," and "French kissing"—all with their calibrated moral penalties. And woe to that person—particularly a Catholic girl—who "went all the way." The chasm of an everlasting hell gaped to receive her and she earned a reputation that fixed her as a pariah among Catholic girls and boys.

That such a rigorous view of sex prevailed among Catholics—not just as an ideal, but as a reality—can be seen in those sex surveys that begin with Alfred Kinsey and continue, proliferating, to our own day. The percentage of those who engaged in premarital sex was considerably lower among Catholics than among other religious groups prior to the 1960s. Attitudes on birth control, abortion, and other moral questions were also much different. During the 1960s and 1970s, however, Catholic moral practices and attitudes became increasingly similar to those of the nation as a whole, much more part of the "norm."

Not every boy who entered the seminary or novitiate and not every girl who entered the convent had rigorously adhered to the Catholic penchant for the most scrupulous sexually moral behavior. (But the incidence of sexually "pure" behavior among girls who entered the convent was probably quite extraordinarily high, reflecting the chivalric, romantic sense of Catholic girlhood that prevailed among Catholics.) I had myself placed my hands on a girl's bare breasts—twice.

How can I describe the horror I felt in the aftermath of these departures from the moral code? When I made my general confession shortly after entering the novitiate, I once again confessed these sins. My mouth was dry. My heart was thumping. I could barely utter the words describing my misdeeds. Would God ever forgive me? To ensure that I would suffer sufficiently here on earth for these heinous sins, I resolved to spend the rest of my life performing additional penances in expiation for having so offended God. When physical penances were announced for novices—the wearing of chains of chicken wire around one's arms and legs for a period of time and the use of the "discipline," a cord whip with which one beat one's bare rump—I would always attempt to wear my chains tighter or beat myself harder in order to mortify my body additionally for my "sins of the flesh."

Such repentance was typical of novices. It was called "first fervor"—a state of exaltation and scrupulous attention to even the smallest detail of the Jesuit rules that all Jesuits, as they grew older, were urged to recreate for themselves. The concept of "modesty of the eyes" was an example of such fervor. "Modesty of the eyes" did not only mean that you avoided feasting your eyes on some bikini-clad model on a billboard, but that you mortified your senses and fostered your interior prayer life by avoiding all distracting viewing.

Certain Jesuit novices would constantly walk around with their eyes lowered, heads bent slightly forward. Others, most notable Brother Brown, practiced "modesty of the eyes" so literally that they shambled along, looking as if their bodies were bent from some spinal disease and almost always careening off a column, some piece of furniture, or another novice.

The piety in the novitiate was quite childlike—a piety fostered by the reading of the lives of the Jesuit "boy saints," three Jesuits who had died quite young "in the odor of sanctity." It was fostered also by the practice that conversations at recreation time be about spiritual topics. In the recreation periods after lunch and supper and on "villa days" (the Thursdays when we hiked to a nearby Jesuit-owned piece of property for a weekly day of recreation), the novices, in their late teens and early twenties, would chatter away about the wonderful attributes of the Blessed Virgin Mary or about how "edified" (a favorite word of Jesuit novices) they were by reading some biography of a saint.

Such seeming extravagance had a certain naive, innocent charm, and was inevitable given the intensive pressure and all-encompassing life of the novitiate. For the two years of Jesuit novitiate, one was not allowed to leave—except for an emergency such as a family death or the necessity for extraordinary medical care. A novice was allowed to write one letter a week to his family and to receive one letter a week from them. No visitors were allowed except one's immediate family—for two hours one Sunday each month.

The "long retreat"—which every Jesuit makes twice during his training, once as a first-year novice, and again in a third year of spiritual training after he has completed his studies—early inspired the Jesuit novice to a zealous fervor. Thirty days long, based on Ignatius Loyola's *Spiritual Exercises*, the "long retreat" was conducted in total silence, except for talks given by the master of novices and for the two days of recreation allowed during this month.

In what was probably the most intensive religious experience of my life, the "long retreat" took me from meditations on hell to contemplation on the love of Christ. One week I would imagine myself dying, a sinner, and would envision the horrors of hell that awaited me. At another time I would meditate on Jesus' life on earth. Probably one of the most profoundly psychological spiritual guides ever devised, the *Spiritual Exercises* made a radical change in almost everyone who used this spiritual process.

The goal for this intensive training was spiritual perfection, saving one's own soul, and saving the souls of others. It was an honorable goal, giving a principle of coherence to one's life. It was the highest goal possible for someone who had grown up Catholic.

Good Friday, 1957, seems a long time ago. My companions on that grassy field at the Novitiate of the Sacred Heart are no longer Jesuits, but instead have gone on to eminent political careers—an indication of the shifting values in U.S. Catholicism. Only the memory lingers—a memory of a brief period in our lives when each of us had responded to what we belived to be a call from God to devote our lives exclusively to Him.

———

The life of U. S. Catholics that existed up to the mid-1960s has, for the most part, disappeared. It has evaporated with the finality of the lost continent of Atlantis, dispersed as completely as Minoan civilization. As with the ancient civilizations of the past, the U.S. Catholic experience has left its archaeological remains: large Gothic churches in cities throughout the country, which today see only a fraction of the worshipers who in decades past filled them, the plaster statues of saints—pejoratively called Sulpician art—that stood in every nook and niche of these churches, the paraphernalia of the liturgy and of the numerous devotions that characterized U.S. Catholic life before the Second Vatican Council—censers that swung with charcoal and incense, monstrances that contained the Blessed Sacrament, mass cards, propped against the altar, which provided the priest with some of the prayers he said while celebrating mass.

Gone, too, are the rituals, the customs, the uniformity that marked Roman Catholicism from the sixteenth to the mid-twentieth centuries. Less than two decades after this way of life came to an end, these rituals and customs are already the subject for the sociologist's investigations and the anthropologist's interpretations.

U.S. Catholicism until the mid-1960s touched almost every aspect of the lives of practicing Catholics. If we posit one-fourth of the population of the United States during the post-World War II period and further speculate that some 60 to 70 percent of nominal Catholics could be accounted practicing Catholics—that is, they followed the minimal dictates that the Church required, attended mass on Sundays and holy days of obligation, abstained from meat on Fridays, and went to confession and Communion once a year—then we view a society as much affected by a religious ethos as Egypt under the Pharaohs.

It was a society that lived by the calendar of the liturgical year, beginning in late November with Advent, that penitential season that ushered in Christmas. After the celebration of Christ's birth, Catholics attended an obligatory mass on New Year's Day to commemorate His circumcision. A few days later, the Feast of the Epiphany recalled the visit of the Magi. Sometime in late winter or early spring, Lent began. Catholics pondered what to "give up" for those forty days. Many would attend daily mass during the few weeks of Lent and the Stations of the Cross on Friday afternoons or evenings. Fasting and abstinence from meat also marked the Lenten season, which began with the awesome Ash Wednesday liturgy and the marking of the foreheads of Catholics with ashes. Then would come the intense, elaborate ritual of Holy Week, rich in symbolism, recreating the institution of the Eucharist and the passion and death of Jesus Christ. Easter brought a joyful close to Lent; and Pentecost began the long, closing liturgical season of the Church.

Feast days—those of Jesus Christ, of the Blessed Virgin Mary, of the saints—punctuated this liturgical season: the Feast of the Sacred Heart of Jesus, Ascension Day, All Saints Day, the Feast of the Immaculate Conception, the Feast of the Assumption, St. Patrick's Day, so dear to Irish-Americans, St. Joseph's Day, held in special reverance by Italian-Americans, St. Boniface's Day, commemorated by German-Americans, St. Stanislaus' Day, celebrated by Polish-Americans.

And if the liturgical cycle of the Church affected the day-to-day rhythm of U.S. Catholics, the parish provided the center for this vitally important religious segment of their lives—and for much of their social lives as well. Catholics in large cities would frequently identify themselves by the parishes in which they lived. "I'm from St. Cecilia's Parish." "I'm from Most Holy Redeemer Parish." Since the parish represented an area with geographical boundaries, it also usually indicated a national and socioeconomic group.

The parish complex ordinarily included the church, a rectory where the priests resided, a grammar school, a parish hall, and a convent where the nuns who taught at the grammar school lived. Presiding over the complex was a pastor, an autocrat in this realm, responsible only to his bishop and assisted by one or more priests. His role—and that of his assistants—was much greater than merely conducting public worship. The parish priests were required to operate every aspect of the parish complex, to bring Communion to the sick, to oversee the parish school, to serve as chaplains and moderators for a myriad of parish organizations and Catholic societies, to counsel parishioners, to bring solace and comfort to those in need, to uphold Catholic morality for their flocks, and to be present at the rites of passage in the life cycles of all those who belonged to the parish—to baptize the newborn, marry young couples, and anoint the dying. During the moments parish priests were able to snatch from these duties, they could be seen wearing their long, black cassocks, walking back and forth in some part of the parish premises, reading the daily liturgical office in Latin from their black-leather breviaries—a duty that took about an hour each day.

The day in the life of a parish priest usually began at dawn or earlier, with the first of two or three daily masses said. It expanded into meetings with contractors to discuss repairs to the church, visits to the sick of the parish, talks to the children at the school, and advice to parishioners who looked to them as psychologists, lawyers, business advisers, counselors. Confessions had to be heard for long hours. Convert classes had to be conducted. Instruction had to be given to those couples about to marry. Baptisms, marriages, and funerals had to be scheduled. The church bulletin had to be printed; and sermons had to be prepared. Planning for the weekly bingo game, the monthly parish potluck dinner, and the annual bazaar had to be considered—for the paster always had to keep in mind the mortgage payments on the buildings within his parish domain. And there were meetings of the Altar Society, the Holy Name Society, the school's Mothers' Guild, and what seemed to be interminable other parish organizations and Catholic societies.

In none of these activities did the pastor or his assistants consult parishioners for advice. It was unthinkable that anyone but the pastor—or, with his permission, the assistant pastors—should participate in the planning, decision-making, or implementation of the decisions that governed parish life. The priests would persistently appeal to the parishioners for funds to support the parish complex, and the parishioners would respond by contributing to the collections at Sunday masses, buying tickets for raffles, attending bingo games, bazaars, and other fund raising events, and being generous with stipends for masses, baptisms, marriages, and funerals. The pastor and his assistants would count every penny of this money, pay the monthly mortgages, maintain the physical plant, pay the expenses of the school, and pay the occasional diocesan assessments. The laity were asked to contribute to and run the bingo games, bazaars, and other such activities; but there ended their participation in the workings of the parish.

Into the parish complex squalling infants were taken shortly after birth to be baptized; and continued, often, to enter the church on Sundays and holy days of obligation as infants and toddlers, brought by parents. Soon they began to come in contact with the religious orders of women—popularly called nuns. Somewhat over fifty per cent of Catholic grammar school children were taught in parochial schools; those who were not were sent to catechetical instruction, which usually began in kindergarten or the first grade. In the first years of grammar school came First Holy Communion—for which each youngster was assiduously prepared by the nuns.

During these growing-up years, Catholic boys and girls were relentlessly drilled in the doctrines and pious practices of Catholicism. They memorized the answers to questions from a series of catechisms. They were urged to say morning and evening prayers, to recite the rosary each day, to wear a holy medal or scapular around their necks, to love and imitate Jesus, Mary, and the saints, and to pray to their guardian angels.

The nuns who taught generations of U.S. Catholics were loved and revered. It was only years later that Catholics who matured in the sexual ambivalence of the 1960s and 1970s began bitter critiques of their teachers' moral rigorism. Before this time, the Catholic community looked upon these women—dressed in the voluminous black habits, which differed with each religious order, and long black, veils or some other distinctive headgear, beneath which shaved heads signified their sacrifice of all things to become "the brides of Christ"—as living saints. They did not have the prestige and authority of priests, though both were celibate. But while parish priests could play golf or go to a movie, the lives of these nuns were centered around their convents or in the Catholic schools, hospitals, and other charitable institutions which they maintained.

The years of adolescence were characterized by a growing awareness of one's sexuality and by the overwhelming efforts of priests, nuns, and brothers to inculcate a rigorous sexual morality. These were also the years to determine whether one had a religious vocation. Large numbers of boys and girls entered novitiates and seminaries after they graduated from the eighth grade; but only a small percentage persevered.

A smaller, but still significant, percentage of Catholics went on to Catholic high schools from parochial grammar schools, and a still smaller percentage attended Catholic colleges. Catholics were strongly urged to attend these schools, despite the educational inferiority of almost all Catholic institutions of higher learning to their secular counterparts. They were bastions of the Faith; whereas other colleges and universities were thought to be places where it was easy to lose one's faith and to sink into immorality.

Marriage was the next rite of passage in which the Church was involved. No Catholic was allowed a civil marriage or a marriage in any church but a Catholic church. The prohibition against any form of birth control was adamant—and followed by the greater percentage of Catholics—and, as a consequence, the Catholic Church in the United States grew substantially.

The married Catholic couple produced children, worked, and passed on the legacy of Catholicism. Men and women both joined Catholic organizations, did their stint for the parish in which they resided, and nurtured their Catholicism during all the vicissitudes of middle age and growing old. Eventually the Catholic died, and his or her body lay in a mortuary where family and friends gathered to say the rosary. The funeral was held in a Catholic church, and burial was frequently in a Catholic cemetery. It was to be hoped that children, relatives, and friends would have masses said to rescue one's soul from the purifying fires of purgatory.

No analysis of U.S. Catholicism before the Second Vatican Council would be complete without a discussion of the impact of immigration on the distinctive features of the Catholic Church in the United States. Since this subject has been written about extensively, it will be discussed only briefly here. The Irish, Polish, German, Slovakian, Lithuanian, and Italian Catholics who came to the United States during the nineteenth and twentieth centuries came into an alien world. With the exception of the Irish, they did not speak English. Virtually all of these immigrants were poor and came from rural areas in Europe. They huddled in enclaves in large cities in the United States, maintaining their national languages and customs, desperately attempting to deal with the discrimination they met in this country. They worked hard at the jobs that were available to them—usually at the lowest end of the economic spectrum. They were ambivalent about the process of assimilation in the society and culture in which they found themselves.

Frequently uneducated and unlettered, from villages in Europe where their Catholicism was taken for granted and was of a simple nature, the immigrants in the United States gravitated to the Church for a complex series of motives. The U.S. Catholic Church was itself beleaguered, and it insured in many ways the retention of some sense of national identity. The parish gave them a sense of comfort and community. The proliferation of parish organizations and Catholic societies provided a social outlet. Catholicism, primarily through the parish structure, seemed to guarantee to the immigrants that they wouldn't be swallowed up and that they wouldn't be devastated by the hostile foreign world in which they lived.

The parish priest, better educated than the immigrant families in his flock, was indeed "the man set apart." He came from the people, but he was not of them. He would use his education, his authority, his power as the head of his flock to protect them, to comfort them, to counsel them, to aid them in their struggles in an alien society.

Nor should one overlook the role of Catholicism in the life of the immigrant—a role which has been a traditional accusation against religion—in palliating the miseries of earthly life with the promise of bliss in the next. For a Slovakian steelworker in a mill in Pittsburgh, for an Irish maid in Boston, for a Polish hog slaughterer in Chicago, for a German brewery worker in Milwaukee, for an Italian ditch-digger in New York, laboring long hours at back-breaking work for very little money, derided and ridiculed by those who were not more immediately "hyphenated Americans," living in crowded, grimy tenements, grappling with a foreign language, struggling to retain a sense of pride and dignity in a complex urban environment, striving to obey laws and regulations they did not understand, the burdens of this life could be intolerable. They could, however, find solace in the comforts of religion. The Church not only provided a sense of nostalgic identification with the past—the villages of Poland, Germany, Italy, and Ireland, and the Slovakian and Hungarian territories of the Austro-Hungarian Empire, it also offered the promise of a blissful future—an eternal one.

As time went on, the sheer pressure of numbers provided political clout. Organized around their parishes, led by their parish priests and the politicians from their national groups, these immigrants began to seek and obtain better jobs: as policemen, auto assembly line workers, truck farmers. This social and economic upward mobility was the result of the tight network of Catholicism centered around the parishes of such cities as Boston, New York, St. Louis, Chicago, Milwaukee, and San Francisco. Father O'Toole would talk to Jim O'Grady, "a good Catholic, an active member of St. Michael's Parish," down in the mayor's office about getting Mrs. O'Rourke's son, Danny, a job in the fire department. Catholic lawyers, doctors, grocers, morticians, shoe repairmen, and clothiers would expect patronage from their coreligionists.

And so developed what has come to be called the "ghetto mentality" of U.S. Catholicism: the twin identification of U.S.

Catholics as being Polish-American, Irish-American, Italian-American and as being Roman Catholic. A fiercely loyal attitude towards the Church developed. The Church, if it did not dominate the lives of Catholics in the United States, was a central, pivotal feature of their existence. It validated them, gave them a sense of pride and dignity, gave them protection and a vehicle for advancing themselves, gave them hope for the future.

This "ghetto mentality" was not only the result of the difficulties of Catholic immigrants with language and customs, with finding jobs, and with a strange environment. It was also the result of an historical hostility of a predominantly Anglo-Saxon Protestant majority against newcomers who happened to be Catholic. The confrontation between Catholicism and Protestantism, after the era of peace and harmony following the Revolution and the early years of the young republic, had its symbolic beginning in 1830 with the founding of *The Protestant*, an openly anti-Catholic weekly newspaper. In the previous decade—the 1820s—some 54,000 Catholics had entered the United States from abroad; and the fear of many Protestants of this rising Catholic immigration, coupled with such increasing problems as sectional rivalry and economic dislocation, caused the latent hostility to Catholicism to break into the open.

The burning down of an Ursuline convent in Charleston, Massachusetts, by an anti-Catholic mob, the notorious "disclosures" of Maria Monk, and the formation of the anti-Catholic political party known as the Know-Nothings are but a few examples of an antagonism and hostility against the growing numbers of European Catholic immigrants in the United States. Similar outbursts of anti-Catholic sentiment took place in the late nineteenth and early twentieth centuries and during the 1920s.

The response among the immigrant Catholics to this hostility was predictable: to live entirely in a Catholic world because you are besieged by those who wish to destroy your faith.

The waves of immigrant Catholics into the United States from the mid-nineteenth century until World War I taxed the energies and the resources of the U.S. Catholic Church to the utmost. It was these masses of new immigrants—crowded for the most part into city slums, generally unable to speak English, seeking jobs in this promised land, frightened of the foreign cultural and technological society in which they were thrust, huddling together in national groups whenever possible in order to ward off homesickness and to seek some security in a frequently hostile and always strange environment—that the Catholic Church in the United States had to bring within its pastoral care; and it was to the Church that these immigrants turned for solace and security. This was to be the profile—a church composed of struggling immigrants—of the Catholic Church in the United States until World War II.

The Catholic immigrants felt that the first duty of parents was to provide religious education for their children; and to accomplish this these immigrants, from their meager incomes and resources, not only built a separate school system but also paid extra tuition to send their children there. The ambitions of Catholics to improve their situation caused the economics of the Catholic school system to become an increasing problem, as did the demands from Rome for more Catholic parish schools. Thus the strain of maintaining Catholic schools and Catholic opposition to the public schools continued to be sources of friction between Catholics and Protestants.

Catholicism in the nineteenth-century United States was not the result of the conversion of a people by missionaries as in the conversion of Western Europe in the Middle Ages, but of the hurried efforts of the Church organization to get priests into the new settlements where the Catholic laity had gone. As a result of this situation, there developed certain characteristics, not all of them positive, which distinguished Catholicism in the United States from that of Europe.

The chief characteristic of U.S. Catholicism was a kind of unquestioning faith. Ordinary Catholic immigrants were too busy acquiring the essentials of a good living to think much about or to study their faith. They depended upon the priest for instruction, and later upon the parish schools to take over the task of teaching their children and inculcating the principles of Catholicism. It seldom occurred to them to question the faith that had given them so much consolation in trial. Despite the differences in language, for the most part there was little difference in the Catholicism that was preached in the churches or taught in the elementary doctrines of the penny catechism.

Although immigration as a source of new Catholics in the United States began to lessen in importance in 1921, when Congress passed the first of a series of immigration restriction laws, the U.S. Catholic Church continued to grow both in numbers and importance of institutions.

Despite this growth—or perhaps because of it—hostility to Catholics continued well into the twentieth century. As a result, there occurred among U.S. Catholic immigrants and their descendants what I call "cultural encapsulization." Being called a "wop," a "dago," a "mick," a "spick," or a "Polak" was part of the demeaning hostility which Catholics encountered in the United States. Since being Italian, Irish, or Polish almost always meant being Catholic, these immigrants retreated into safe ethnic/religious ghettos. The Church became for them a bastion against the barbs of this unfriendly society.

This "cultural encapsulization" among Catholics is illustrated by the dedication in the 1949 St. Ignatius High School yearbook. This San Francisco Jesuit high school was typical of many metropolitan high schools. Its students were the children and grandchildren of immigrants, a diverse ethnic mix, and part of an emerging, increasingly affluent middle class. The dedication reads as follows:

> Going forth into a hostile and pagan world
> Surrounded on all sides by old errors revamped as new
> Disguised as lately discovered truths
>> Surrounded by a hypocritical world that
>> Is afraid to defy God
>> And so disregards and laughs at Him . . .
>> It is well that the young men of the Class of '49
> Recognize as their particular patron
> The Saint that is the teacher of their teachers
> Who also was tempted to sophistication
>> But who rose to sanctity in a world of sin
>> So to Saint Ignatius Loyola, servant of Jesus,
>> We dedicate this journal of our activities
>> In the hope that through his intercession with
> Mary and with Jesus
> We of the Class of '49 may remain ever steadfast
> In our Holy Faith.

Even accounting for the youthful ardor of high school graduates, such a dedication was written in 1949, thirteen years before the Second Vatican Council began, by a group of students for whom the rigors, economic and social, of being immigrants had already begun to recede.

It was as a response to these twin challenges—uprooting themselves from Europe and settling in a strange, harsh environment, and having to face the hostility of older and non-Catholic settlers in the United States—that Catholics became forged into a hermetic, tightly-knit community that expressed itself in a heightened spirituality and a fierce loyalty to the Roman Catholic Church.

This was an era when the football victories of Notre Dame University were greeted with jubilation by Catholics throughout the United States, when the election of James Michael Curley as mayor of Boston was looked upon as a political coming of age for Catholics, when the appointment of James Farley to a cabinet post was thought to be yet another step toward the goal of Catholics being accepted as equals.

This was an era when Catholic societies and organizations provided for virtually every facet of one's life on earth—from insurance to playing sports. This was an era when one listened with conscious pride and loyalty to the broadcasts of Fulton J. Sheen, to the "Rosary Hour," to the "Catholic Hour"; when one subscribed to the *Extension*, the *Messenger of the Sacred Heart*, the *Liguorian*, and one's diocesan newspaper.

This was an era when not eating meat on Fridays was the proud badge of being a Catholic, when fasting on Ember Days and Rogation Days was a matter of course, when Catholic marriages almost always ended only when one of the parties died, and when one had all the children "that God sent."

This was an era when Catholicism touched every aspect of a Catholic's life from the cradle to the grave, gave it an imprint that was both a fascination and a vague repulsion to U.S. citizens who were not Catholics, an era of Our Lady of Perpetual Help devotions. . . .

This was an era which would end in the 1960s with the suddenness and finality of Pompei.[6]

# 3| The Making and Unmaking of the *Jubilee* Catholic

The year was 1958. A freshman at the Jesuit-operated University of San Francisco climbed the stairs to the nearby San Francisco College for Women, the elegant college run by the Madames of the Sacred Heart. He noticed an attractive young woman reading a magazine on the lawn in front of the castle-like building.

"Hi. Are you reading *Jubilee*?" he inquired.

It was with these words that author and critic Kevin Starr met the woman who would become his wife. And the question was indicative of the young Catholic men and women who had discovered new dimensions in Catholicism during the 1950s and early 1960s.

In reality, the short-lived intellectual and aesthetic Catholicism in the United States that I describe as "*Jubilee* Catholicism"—and which has also been described as "Commonwealth Catholicism" and "Fifties Catholicism"—had its roots in the 1930s and its beginnings in the metropolitan centers of New York and Chicago. In New York, the start of *Commonweal* in 1924 and the *Catholic Worker* in the mid-1930s would articulate a Catholic voice that was both liberal and intellectual. The vision of the founders of *Commonweal* as a magazine that would deal with serious political, social, and artistic issues—a magazine owned and operated by laypersons—resulted in one of the most influential Catholic publications in the United States for the next four decades. Much of its influence arose from a combination of "old-line" Catholic intellectuals, and from a new generation of Catholics who were emerging from the limitations of immigrant ghettos in cities throughout the United States.[1]

The *Catholic Worker* and its attendant Catholic Worker Movement—the result of the commitment to pacifism and social justice on the part of its founders, Dorothy Day and Peter Maurin—was yet another sign of the ferment and change within U.S. Catholicism.

Chicago in the 1930s was the other pole of influence that would have a major impact on U.S. Catholicism. Andrew Greeley writes:

> In the late 1930s there began in the archdiocese of Chicago a series of experiments that would anticipate in many respects the spirit and teachings of the Vatican Council. These experiments in lay action, social action, catechetics, liturgy, and marriage education would be imitated all over the United States, and the men who began them would become national figures and the heroes of many of the progressive Catholics of the country.[2]

The 1930s were a period of social and economic ferment. The New Deal's attempts to mitigate the effects of the Great Depression were reflected by Catholics in Chicago—both lay and clergy—who proclaimed a social action gospel and founded organizations to deal with the social and economic problems of the times. Armed with the social encyclicals of Popes Leo XIII and Pius XI, men such as Monsignor John Ryan, Bishop Bernard Sheil, Martin Carrabine, S.J., Edward Marciniak, James O'Gara, John Cogley, and Jerome Kerwin attempted to deal with this social and economic ferment through the application of Catholic principles. Monsignor Reynold Hillenbrand was probably the most important of those who sought at this time to effect the synthesis that would become known as "the church in the modern world."

From the activities of these men and others, a host of organizations evolved in Chicago that were to have a major impact on post-World War II Catholicism in the United States. The first Cana Conference was held in Chicago. Friendship House, a lay spiritual community, was opened under the direction of Baroness Katherine De Hueck Doherty. The Grail, another lay community, made its first foundation in the United States near Liberty-ville, Illinois.The Sheil School of Social Studies provided some of the intellectual stimulus that was needed in the midst of so much activity. The Catholic Labor Alliance and the Catholic Interracial Council were formed. Catholic action groups began to appear in Catholic high schools and colleges as well as among Catholic businessmen, the businessmen's wives, and also young working people. The Christian Family Movement began in the late 1940s. In 1948 Dan Herr became associated with the Thomas More Bookstore, and the bookstore and its magazine *Books on Trial* (later *The Critic*) became an important part of the Chicago scene.

The Chicago experience—and its counterpart in New York—represented a new era in U.S. Catholicism, an era that was characterized by certain social and economic phenomena that were to change radically the profile of the U.S. Catholic. The labor struggles of the 1930s and 1940s, and the affluence triggered by World War II and its expansionist aftermath, brought greater prosperity to millions of Catholics. No longer were Catholic immigrants and their children and grandchildren a marginal group, struggling for an economic "place in the sun." Further, new generations of Catholics had been born in the United States, spoke English as a first language, and, as a result of post-World War II mobility and the greater economic opportunities open to them, began to move out of the immigrant ghettos in which they had grown up. Along with the new times came greater educational opportunities and a greater impetus toward higher education. Thousands upon thousands of the sons and daughters of barely literate immigrant parents and grandparents went to college and graduate and professional schools during the 1940s, 1950s, and 1960s.

For this growing segment of U.S. Catholics, particularly those attending Catholic colleges and universities, the two decades following the end of World War II were a period of transition. Assimilation into the mainstream of U.S. culture was a developing process. Moves out of immigrant ghettos into more fashionable urban residential sections and into the suburbs lessened the influence of ethnic enclaves. There was much less identification with the traditions of the "old country." And yet some identification remained. Even college-educated men and women, who were now taking jobs as governmental bureaucrats, attorneys, and businesspersons, continued to identify themselves as Irish-Americans, Italian-Americans, Polish-Americans. Increasing intermarriage between ethnic groups did not materially diminish this identification. Nor did the fact that many found themselves in more heterogeneous neighborhoods—both ethnically and religiously—than those they had previously experienced.

When my parents moved to the San Francisco suburb of San Mateo in 1953, for example, they sought and found much of the same Italian-American life they had left. It was less "old country" than South San Francisco—fewer old immigrants lived there—and my parents had more social contact with those who were not of Italian parentage. And the ranch-style house they built was less obviously the working class, immigrant house that my grandmother and grandfather had built in the 1920s. But the template of Italian-American—and Catholic—life was imposed on their new surroundings.

If ethnic identification remained strong despite greater assimilation in the pluralism of the United States, these new generations descended from Catholic immigrants found even greater identification in the Catholic Church.

It was that minority element of the Catholic population, which sought out educational opportunities and gravitated to the professions, to middle and upper managerial positions in corporations, and to academic posts, that would characterize *Jubilee* Catholicism during the two decades following the end of World War II.

If one were to describe this movement, particularly during its heyday in the 1950s and early 1960s, it would be seen as politically and socially liberal, open to European theological influences, and in revolt against the "ghetto mentality" of U.S. Catholicism. The political and social liberalism that marked the post-World War II years was probably an organic outgrowth of the bread-and-butter liberalism of parents and grandparents, and of the adherence of most U.S. Catholics to the Democratic

Party, forged in the earlier struggles that had marked the immigrants' social and economic battles. New Deal liberalism had buttressed this affinity; and the papal social encyclicals had provided a religious and intellectual foundation. The combination of greater affluence, which allowed many Catholics relative freedom from economic concerns and greater educational opportunities, and the intellectual and cultural ferment that—paradoxically—marked the "apathetic Fifties," stimulated the intellectual and artistic facets of this aspect of post-war Catholicism. This in turn led to a rebellion against the continuing antiintellectual, clerically dominated, ethnically inspired Catholic Church in the United States.

As a backdrop for this rebellion, one must view the tensions and ambivalences in the U.S. Catholic Church in the post-World War II period. Loyalty to the Church had been intensified as a result of the Church's advocacy of the labor movement. This loyalty had overflowed to virtually every activity of the Church's life. For example, in the early part of the twentieth century, the U.S. Church began to contribute both funds and missionaries to the foreign missions; and today the Catholic Church in the United States is one of the mainstays of these foreign missions—in the contribution of funds as well as of missionaries.

There has been an abatement of concern for missionary activity in the U.S. Catholic Church during the post conciliar era. However, my memory continues to hold images of the importance of the foreign missions during my youth. Sermons urging contributions to the foreign missions were frequently heard in churches, usually delivered by missionaries on "begging" tours in the United States. Catholic children were urged by the nuns who taught them to save their pennies, nickels, and dimes to "buy pagan babies." (This process is still a mystery to me and my contemporaries. Were children really purchased? Or was this only a metaphor for use with children? And, why did pagan baby boys cost twice the amount of pagan baby girls?)

In the 1950s, missionaries returning from torture and imprisonment in China gave the U.S. Catholic Church a feeling of connection with the heroic martyrs of the past. Millions of Catholics listened with rapt attention as missionary after missionary told tales of how the Chinese communists—the new Roman persecutors—had uprooted and destroyed the Church in China.

Such accounts fueled the anticommunist inclinations of U.S. Catholics. Once again, the need of U.S. Catholics to prove their patriotism was a principal motivation for Catholic support of anticommunist activities—coupled with the intensity of feeling provoked by tales of Catholic missionaries being tortured and imprisoned; the banning of the Church in such formerly Catholic countries as Hungary, Poland, and Czechoslovakia; and the mockery of justice in the trial of the Hungarian prelate, Josef Cardinal Mindzenty. For most Catholics, these were matters not only of political ideology, but also personal battles in an area of great importance—their Catholic faith.

I can still remember buying a comic book from the nuns who taught me catechism, shortly after Mindzenty's trial was over, which depicted the heroic struggle of this primate of Hungary: his brainwashing and his kangeroo trial. The tortures of Mindzenty and the oppression of the Catholic Church in Hungary deeply impressed me, and created a strong antipathy to the godless communist persecutors.

The symbol of the conservatism in U.S. Catholicism in the postwar years was the powerful archbishop of New York, Francis Cardinal Spellman. A "super-patriot" in his role as Military Ordinary and in his rigorous defense of the military activities of the United States, he took an active role in organizing support and maintaining a lobby for the anticommunist activities of the U.S. government. The *bête noire* of social liberals for his action in dispatching seminarians to work during a strike of cemetery workers in a Catholic cemetery, Spellman also sought to protect the morals of Catholics by leading the attack on the showing of certain movies, such as "The Miracle," "The Moon Is Blue," and "Baby Doll," as offensive to public morals.

Father McAvoy summarized the Catholic experience in the United States during this period:

> The life of American Catholicism in the years after the war was that of a loosely formed giant awakening from a sleep, each part of which had grown to tremendous size and was beginning to move one member at a time to see if they were really viable. Lo-

cal censuses indicated that there were more Catholics in the country than anyone realized but that not all of them were at Mass every Sunday. The estimates of attendance at Sunday Mass ranged as high as sixty-five percent on the average in some tabulations, much less in others. New churches and schools were being built, but not enough schools to take care of the increased Catholic population and of those children whose parents had returned to the Church during the war. One important development in the movement to suburbia was the interest in the liturgy manifested by these families, particularly by younger families. The first great victory of the liturgical movement in the era was the restoration of the old Holy Week rites, but there was also a growing use of translated missals by the people attending Mass. There was an increasing number of Catholic books published and a few Catholic books reached the best-seller market, such as Thomas Merton's *The Seven Story Mountain* and some books by Bishop Fulton J. Sheen and Fulton Oursler. While Catholic publications did not reach a wide public, there was a noticeable catering to Catholics by such widely circulated periodicals as *Life* and *Time.* . . . Catholic publications, books, or periodicals were read by a minority of a minority. The Catholic weekly newspapers, subsidized by the local Ordinary, had wide circulation when all the subscribers were added together, but they had little influence on the general public.[3]

This lack of influence of the Catholic press and the mediocrity of Catholic periodicals and books mirrored an intellectual impoverishment among U.S. Catholics that was largely the result of the recent-immigrant status of the Church in the United States. However, the proliferation of Catholic institutions of higher learning, most of them poorly endowed, almost all of them mediocre or worse, did not aid the cause of Catholic scholarship. George Shuster, president of New York's Hunter College, had discussed this issue as early as 1925. But it was Monsignor John Tracy Ellis' essay of criticism in 1955 (and a critique by Gustave Weigel, S.J., in 1957) that sparked intense debate and controversy during the late 1950s.[4] Many joined the chorus of criticism of Catholic cultural and educational efforts; but little of practical value seemed to be accomplished as a result of the self-appraisal.

During the second half of the 1950s, I attended one of these "mediocre or worse" Catholic colleges—the University of San Francisco. If my memory serves me correctly, it was one of *nine*

Catholic institutions of higher learning that served the San Francisco Bay Area. Philosophy courses were badly taught expositions of neo-Thomism, using as a textbook a manual by a Brother Benignus, which set up non-Thomist philosophers as strawmen; and one had only to memorize a few deft answers to refute their philosophical systems. So-called theology courses were little better than advanced catechetics, taught mostly by Jesuits who were either alcoholics or distinctly inferior scholars and teachers. Each student was required to take one course in both philosophy and theology each quarter.

What saved this academic experience for me—and for countless other Catholic students in Catholic colleges—was the occasional outstanding scholar and teacher who combined his or her talent with an apostolic zeal that could fire our imaginations. And since most Catholic colleges had a relatively small enrollment, relationships with such teachers could easily develop.

A feature of U.S. Catholicism in the post-World War II period was the diaspora from the inner city to the suburb. This phenomenon, which Catholics shared with many others in the United States, indicated some major socioeconomic changes among U.S. Catholics; principally, greater affluence and greater assimilability. The economic effects of World War II and its aftermath created a substantial middle class of what had but a few years before been masses of economically marginal immigrant workers.

This affluence, coupled with the correlative move out of the ethnic neighborhoods of inner cities that had been such bastions—or ghettos—of Polish, or Irish, or German, or Italian Catholics, into the more heterogeneous suburbs, was to create a new experience for Catholics in the United States. And even when the suburbs were transplants of former urban ethnic neighborhoods, there were key differences: the Catholic suburbanites were two—and often three—generations removed from immigrant status; they were better educated and more sophisticated; unlike their parents and grandparents, they no longer identified the Church as their protector from the fears and anxieties of living in a strange land. It was this new genre of Catholics that would face the social, intellectual, and religious ferment of the 1960s and 1970s.

Probably the best description of this movement in U.S. Catholicism is contained in Garry Wills' *Bare Ruined Choirs.* Wills writes:

> How escape the parish while remaining a loyal son of Mother Church? The Catholic liberal responded with a theological equivalent of the higher patriotism: a higher churchiness, the style of a believing critic. He would be the *true* churchman of doctrine and liturgy—just as liberals throughout the country were the true patriots, fighting McCarthy's caricature love of country and "superpatriotism." The Catholic liberal would be more in love with incense than any altar boy; yet he would intellectualize his incense in a congenial setting. He made ceremony less vulgar by making it even more exotic. It was not Rome he disliked in his churches; it was Peoria.[5]

The movement was more than the "revolt in matters of taste" that Wills and theologian George Devine describe as characterizing this period and segment of U.S. Catholicism.[6] It was also the attempt of younger Catholics—newly liberated from the narrow parochialism of the Catholic ethnic ghetto, emancipated from the grosser forms of prejudice and bigotry, freed from the driving necessities of economic survival, plunged into the delicious experience of a liberal college education—to discover a new Catholic identification, an identification rooted in the broad intellectual and cultural mainstream of the Catholic tradition which would provide them with a distinctive sense of Catholicity in the pluralistic culture of the United States.

Wills discusses some of the specifics that separated this "new breed" of U.S. Catholic from his forebears and from the mainstream of U.S. Catholicism. He writes:

> The liberal became more an "old world" Catholic than his parish priest, going back to a romantic past in order to escape the cloddish present, to forge a possible future for educated Catholics. This kind of liberal liked to slip off on weekends to some monastery—to Tom Merton's Gethsemane, where he could rise in the middle of the night and listen to Trappists (silent at other times) chanting their "hours"; or to St. John's Abbey in Minnesota, where he might run into Gene McCarthy or his wife, Abigail (who reviewed books for the house liturgical journal, *Wor-*

*ship);* or to a retreat house, where he could observe monastic silence."[7]

It is obvious today that much of this revolt from "ghetto Catholicism" had a great deal to do with the eagerness of one generation to escape from the authority of the older generation and to establish its own identification. This was especially true in immigrant Catholic families, where traditionally strong parental rule could be offset with a certain disdain by children cognizant of their superior education and improved job possibilities. A sense of superiority—and therefore a certain sense of independence—could be achieved against both parents and priests (the latter were strong authority figures in Catholic parishes) by cultivating an "enlightened Catholicism." The constraints and restrictions of a ghetto community, where many Catholic boys and girls grew up dreaming of escaping from the banal, often insensitive and unintellectual, existence of their working class, immigrant parents and neighbors, could be exorcised by creating a more fulfilling aesthetic and intellectual Catholicism—one not identified with that form of Catholicism practiced by their parents, preached in bad sermons by the priests at church, or taught in simplistic terms by the nuns.

The "new breed" Catholics—or Catholic liberals, to use Wills' descriptive phrase—owned a missal in which they followed the mass in English (and, in many cases, in Latin). No daydreaming, reciting the rosary, or reading devotional prayers for these Catholics during the liturgy. They often went to daily mass and were frequent communicants. In many cases, Catholic liberals owned a breviary, and, in imitation of priests and monks, would partake in the "opus Dei"—the daily liturgical "hours" of the Church.

The tradition of French Catholicism for the liberal Catholics replaced that of the English Catholic apologists of the earlier twentieth century. Authors such as G.K. Chesterton, Hillaire Belloc, and Christopher Hollis gave way to Leon Bloy, Georges Bernanos, François Mauriac, and Charles Peguy. Jacques Maritain and Etienne Gilson were the favorite philosophers. The "in" theologians were the Jesuits Danielou and De Lubac and the Dominicans Congar and Chenu. These four men also had the advantage—in the eyes of Catholic liberals—of being anathemized by the conservative curialists in Rome. Guéranger, Gelineau, and Marmion provided liturgical insights. *Monsieur Vincent* and *Diary of a County Priest* were movies that Catholic liberals saw again and again. No enthusiastic reception for *The Bells of St. Mary's*, *Going My Way*, or *Come to the Stable* for them. The journal *Cross Currents* translated key existentialist texts from the French; and after reading these, Catholic liberals could in turn read Sertillanges' classic book, *The Intellectual Life*, Régamey on the ideal of Christian art, and Mersch on the "Mystical Body."

Catholic liberals of the post-World War II period were acutely conscious of their minority position in U.S. Catholicism. The bishops and priests—most of them—exasperated Catholic liberals. On the other hand, as Garry Wills describes the paradox of the Catholic liberals' position:

> . . . The liberal was not really fighting Rome. He opposed the American church because it was all too American. Its bishops had been shaped more by the ethos of the local chamber of commerce than by the American Academy in Rome. The pastor was obnoxious, not for his theology or his transnational ties, but for his lack of theology and parochialism. He was Babbitt in a biretta—as (conversely) Billy Graham was Fulton Sheen in a business suit.[8]

Medievalism and monasticism provided the fundamental cast of the liberal Catholic's religious and intellectual life. Neo-Thomism became the philosophical underpinning of this intellectual life. Maritain was responsible for the rediscovery of neo-Thomism. The "hours" would frequently be recited by several Catholic liberals together. In 1950, when Robert Hoyt (later the founder of the *National Catholic Reporter*) founded a Catholic daily, the *Sun Herald*, the staff attempted communal life and said the breviary together. Carol Jackson, the editor of *Integrity*, wished to "Catholicize" everyday life. She proposed starting a Catholic restaurant, to be called "The Refectory," which would serve a macrobiotic diet—one which was both natural and "spiritual." (Such a plan would later be successfully accomplished by the Zen Center in San Francisco and other Eastern spiritual groups.)

This romanticization of medievalism and monasticism was very much a rebellion against the harsh angularity of the Industrial Age (as such movements often are—for example, those of William Morris and Eric Gill in nineteenth-century England) and the barrenness of the parish life in U.S. Catholicism. The simpler life of the Middle Ages, the use of the arts for worship, and the Catholic aspect of everyday life were in sharp contrast to the parish priest's unintelligibly mumbled Latin at mass, banal sermons, the singing by choir or congregation of a saccharine repertoire of hymns, and Sulpician art—those plaster statues and pictures that profaned the churches. Thus Catholic liberals sought out the monasteries to see what *real* liturgical ceremonies looked like, unearthed obscure rites and signs from Dom Prosper Gueranger's fifteen-volume *Liturgical Year*, and bought records of Gregorian chant by the monks of Solesmes. The Ikon Guild would send them Eastern Orthodox chants or the African "Missa Luba," with tom-toms punctuating the Latin *Gloria*. At bookstores such as the Junipero Serra Shop in San Francisco, Catholic liberals could buy driftwood-swirl Madonnas, wrought iron abstract tracery for the Stations of the Cross, and brightly colored tapestries of angular representations of saints. The liturgical aesthetic consciousness of Catholic liberals led them to decry the sham Gothic parish churches and diocesan cathedrals (although they praised the authentically Gothic cathedrals and churches of Europe), to seek a more cup-like chalice (in the case of liberal priests) than the sterile goblet-like ones in use, and to advocate that priests wear long surplices and long, flowing chasubles rather than the skimpy, U-shaped type worn at most parish masses.

The monastic strain in liberal Catholicism stressed the idea of a "priesthood of the laity," as Garry Wills points out.[9] Since their parish priests were uninspiring as spiritual mentors, Catholic liberals needed to believe that liturgical functions could be performed outside of the stifling, barren atmosphere of their parish church.

They could follow the saintly (but tough-minded) Dorothy Day's lead and recite the breviary and sing austere Latin hymns. They could read *Integrity*, which ran such articles as "Our Work

Can Help Us to Pray," "Interior Stance," and "Why Aren't Americans Contemplative?" The enthusiasts at places like Grailville could encourage Catholic liberals in new ways to observe the liturgical year at home with advent wreaths, by houses darkened for Lent, with eggs decorated with the Chi-Rho anagram for Christ, a Lamb of God replacing the Easter bunny in candy baskets, light shows at Christmas, and Mary shrines in May. Such a liturgy in the home compensated for the drab hour spent Sunday morning at the parish mass. Catholic liberals used ancient symbols, such as the fish on stationery and the chancery hand while writing letters, in everyday life. They could read *Jubilee* to learn how to make the Christmas tree a "Jesse tree," and *Worship* on how the father of the house should bless it. *Integrity* made up liturgical games for children; and Mary Reed Newland's 1956 book, *The Year and Your Children*, taught mothers what to do on each of the twelve days of Christmas, how to make "God Loves You" valentines, and how to climax the liturgical year in Holy Week by making a Jonah with his whale: on Good Friday Jonah is placed in the whale, and on Easter Sunday the first child awake runs downstairs to take him out again, "resurrected."

It was assumed by many at the time of the Second Vatican Council and its aftermath that the sweeping liturgical changes which occurred—particularly those which decreed the vernacular liturgy—were prompted by liberal Catholics. This was not the case. The pioneering liturgical journal in the United States, *Worship* (formerly called *Orate Fratres*), had cautiously suggested *some* use of English in "the Mass of the Catechumens" (what is now referred to as "the Service of the Word"). As late as 1959, speakers at the Liturgical Week were asked, ahead of time, not to bring up the subject of English in the mass—it would be too controversial. In the same year, *Jubilee* ran an article on the Gelineau method of chanting psalms in the vernacular; the author assured his audience that to think of this as "tantamount to a wish to rival, even to supplant, the Latin Psalter and the Gregorian tones, is to misunderstand" the ancillary uses first proposed for such non-Latin forms. Several months later the magazine called Gregorian chant "the voice of Christ in His mystical body."

No, Catholic liberals did not wish Latin to be supplanted by English in the Church's liturgical life. Latin, after all, was the continuing expression of the Middle Ages; and Gregorian chant was the most important liturgical adjunct for Catholic liberals. Wills writes:

> They knew their chant, and could talk of modes and cadences, of "neumatic" and "melismatic," of "concentus" and "accentus," of chironomy and "the Solesmes theory." They discussed the relative merits of the best chant performers—Solesmes, say, against Taize in France; St. John's against St. Meinrad's in America. Merton had given the importance of chant his imprimatur. Choirmasters in Catholic colleges read *The Gregorian Review.*... Manhattanville, the toniest Catholic girls school, had a special institute, the Pius X School of Liturgical Music, devoted to Gregorian authenticity.[10]

Latin words were used with abandon by Catholic liberals. Somehow this "dead" language seemed to connote religion—Catholicism. Communities took names like *Caritas* or *Domus Dominae* (Baroness de Hueck's Canadian establishment). A printing venture was called *Fides* Press. A peace organization was named *Pax Christi*. A musical journal was not only named after the patron saint of music, but given the patron's name in its Latin form, *Caecilia*. And, when Catholic liberals were not using Latin, they might substitute Italian, as in the *Pio Decimo* Press or the *Studio Angelico* Art School. Even a journal that *seemed* to have an English title, *Mediator*, was actually just the first word from Pius XII's Latin encyclical on the liturgy, *Mediator Dei*. The liturgist's songbook Latinized the Greek invocation of the mass, and was called a *Kyriale*.

Catholic liberals did not, however, look only to the past for their identification with a great and glorious heritage, even though Walsh's *The Thirteenth—Greatest of the Centuries* was read by virtually every Catholic liberal at some time during his or her academic training. The *"Jubilee* Catholic" sought to make Catholic orthodoxy both respectable and first-rate. Thus, the Jesuit Gerard Manley Hopkins was lauded for his ability to escape the confines of nineteenth-century English poetry. (Catholic liberals were usually well-versed on such literary-metaphysical concepts as Hopkins' "inscape" and the influence on him by the medieval philosopher Duns Scotus.) Catholic aesthetes reveled in the modern literary masterpieces that gave a theological interpretation to life. No book was more praised, for example, than Sigrid Undset's *Kristin Lavransdatter*.

Nor was the reading list parochially narrowed to authors who were practicing Catholics. Christopher Fry, T. S. Eliot, and C. S. Lewis were read and praised as being in the "Catholic" tradition.[11]

This consciousness of "Catholic" literary production extended also to works of non-fiction. Maritain's *Art and Scholasticism*, for example, was the main intellectual guide for Thomas Merton as he came into the Church. Christopher Dawson's *The Making of Europe* was recommended to every Catholic college undergraduate who showed any propensity to become a Catholic intellectual.

Another feature that characterized Catholic liberals was their enthusiasm for papal encyclicals. Just as they had worked out an escape from a dreary parish liturgy by fashioning an intellectual approach to Catholicism through neo-Thomism, the French theologians, and a pursuit of modern literature and art, Catholic liberals could appeal to a higher *authority* in ecclesiastical matters through the use of the encyclicals.[12]

In liturgical matters, for example, Catholic liberals could point to—and usually quote—Pius XII's *Mediator Dei* as the document which supported his delight in correctly performed liturgical services and in the use of Gregorian chant. Pius XII's thoughts on the liturgy, said Catholic liberals, were the statement of the Church: the bishops and priests of the United States were far from observing them.

Even more extensively used by Catholic liberals were the *Rerum Novarum* of Leo XIII and *Quadragesimo Anno* of Pius XI. These two encyclicals were *par excellence* the "social encyclicals" of the Church—and the founding documents of Catholic liberalism. Their rather European flavor could not be acclimatized in the United States; so Catholic liberals interpreted them in a way that favored the social and economic principles and legislation that flowed out of the New Deal. Although the two documents were probably in large part inspired by anti-Masonic and anti-Marxist fervor in Rome, they proved capable of great elasticity in the United States.

These encyclicals—as interpreted by Catholic liberals in the United States—advantageously combined the adherence of most Catholics to the Democratic Party with the antiIndustrial Age, communitarian biases of the Catholic liberal. Thus, *Rerum Novarum* and *Quadragesimo Anno* were used to support legislation that abolished child labor, enacted minimum wages, protected small merchants, broke up monopolies, safeguarded private property as the bastion of the family unit, and revived farm life. In this way, the encyclicals could be used to make the Church appear socially progressive and yet avoid the excesses of communism.

In another way, they could be used by medieval-leaning Catholic liberals in their criticism of the city, materialism, and mechanization Monsignor Ligutti's Catholic Rural Life Conference, Peter Maurin's "green revolution," and the Central-Verein (an organization of German Catholics in the Midwest) version of grangerism were examples of this yearning for what the Catholic liberal considered the economic ideals of the Middle Ages. So were the communitarian experiments that abounded in the post-World War II years: Grail Farm, Peter Maurin Farm, Maryfarm, Friendship House, Joe Hill House, Caritas House, Siloe House, the Houses of Hospitality.

Yet another surge of praise for papal encyclicals would come in 1961 when Pope John XXIII issued *Mater et Magistra*, and two years later at the time of *Pacem in Terris*. Coinciding with the years in office of the first Catholic ever to be elected president of the United States, these two encyclicals may have marked the apogee of the U.S. Catholic liberal.

If the religious characteristics discussed above distinguished the "new breed" of Catholic in the postwar years, what were those aspects of traditional U.S. Catholicism that they viewed with disfavor? There is no question here of any doctrinal dispute; nor does the question imply that Catholic liberals would not go to mass on Sunday—despite the drab liturgy—or that they would question the Church's teachings on birth control or on other matters. There was little in matters of "faith and morals" that separated Catholic liberals from those Catholics who were content with the liturgy in the parish church, happy with membership in the Knights of Columbus or the Catholic Daughters of America, and who participated in the life of the parish by volunteering to help at the monthly bingo game or the annual bazaar. Catholic liberals might pity those poor benighted Catholics who continued to light a candle in front of a plaster statue of St. Anthony when they had lost something, who believed that the pastor and the bishop were always correct in their pronouncements and were to be revered as somehow above the layperson, who didn't go off on retreat to a Trappist monastery, and didn't read *Commonweal*, *Worship*, and *Jubilee*; but, however they might differ in their intellectual and aesthetic concepts of Catholicism, both Catholic liberals and their nonliberal coreligionist went to mass on Sundays and holy days of obligation, believed in theory Catholics shouldn't practice birth control, went to confession, accepted the doctrine of the Immaculate Conception and the Assumption of the Blessed Virgin Mary, and, in general, were fundamentally loyal to the traditional teachings of the Church.

The differences—aside from the intellectual and aesthetic aspects described above—were in large part those of Catholic liberals' disdain for the crudities of the typical parish and uninspired leadership of the typical bishop. The increasingly well-educated Catholic laity deplored what they considered the ignorance, the lack of intellectual and artistic taste, and the seemingly exclusive concern for administrative matters that marked the ordinary parish priest and diocesan bishop. Theirs was not the simple faith of the immigrants, looking to the parish and the parish priest for comfort and sustenance in an alien land. Catholic liberals, comfortable as citizens of the United States, increasingly affluent, and reasonably well-educated, felt they had outgrown the Church of the immigrant ghettos.

One of the aspects of "ghetto Catholicism" of which Catholic liberals disapproved was the proliferation of devotions to the Virgin Mary and the saints. Liberals believed Catholic doctrine on both Mary and the saints and manifested devotion to them, but felt that this devotion should be put in perspective. Their major complaint was that popular devotion took away from proper liturgical worship—as when Catholics said the rosary or read devotional prayers during mass. The liberals therefore tended to play down such phenomena as Lourdes or Fatima, First Fridays and First Saturdays, and other such "extra-liturgical" events. In all likelihood, however, these devotions probably reminded them too much of their own youth in the narrow, confining un-intellectualism of growing up Catholic.

Catholic liberals also objected to the popular religious revivalism that marked the U.S. Catholic Church in the 1940s and 1950s—both in the parish and on a national basis.[13] This was the era of Father Feeney and Father Lord, of Father Peyton and Father Keller, of Monsignor (later Archbishop) Fulton J. Sheen and of Fulton Oursler. These men, with their simple religious and moral crusading ardor, filled the newspapers, radio, and television with their calls for a religious reawakening. Father Peyton urged Catholics to say the rosary daily. Father Keller's Christopher Movement urged Catholics to be forces for good in everyday life. Father Lord crusaded for sexual purity.

The parishes had their own versions of these religious crusades. At least once a year a visiting priest—selected for his fire-and-brimstone oratory—would spend nine days in a parish as part of a "circuit-riding" series of novenas. Catholics in the parish would be urged to attend mass and go to communion daily for these nine days of novena. The visiting priest would preach at the mass and would deliver a long sermon in the evening, calling on the parishioners to reform their lives. The singing of hymns and benedictions also characterized each evening of these calls to "reform and renewal." For Catholic liberals the novenas —as well as their national media counterparts—smacked of fundamentalism and revivalism. They were a continuation of the blind, unquestioning faith of ghetto Catholicism. Liberals scorned the parish priests for allowing "bad" art in the churches, conducting uninspired liturgical ceremonies, giving absurd sermons, and being concerned only with the practical aspects of parish administration, and then expecting a full religious life to develop in the parish as a result of nine days of dramatic oratory, rosary-reciting, and benediction.

The ways in which Catholic liberals escaped what they considered these crudities have been described above. Their inspiration for new ways to express his Catholicism was a monthly magazine which best reflected this era of liberal Catholicism—*Jubilee*. Typical Catholic liberals probably read the austerely designed *Commonweal*. They also may have read *Liturgical Arts* and *Worship*; and, depending on their specific interests, other publications. However, it was *Jubilee* that best characterized the yearnings of the new breed of Catholic.

Founded in 1953, *Jubilee* had a format reminiscent of *Time Magazine*. Layout and design tried to approximate that of *Life*. Several feature articles in each issue—almost all of them illustrated with photographs and other graphics—offered a varied fare to Catholic liberals. It reflected a fascination with Eastern Orthodoxy and the Eastern Catholic rites. Monastic groups throughout the world were written about and their environments photographed. Most issues had articles on various saints or Catholics of extraordinary holiness: St. Jerome, Charles de Foucauld, Edith Stein. Catholic communal groups were yet another subject of interest. Catholic literature and virtually every aspect of liturgical art were extensively covered.

*Jubilee* was probably the most important influence on developing the distinctive spirituality and refined taste of Catholic liberals during the 1950s and early 1960s. The magazine's financial decline in the mid-1960s and its demise in 1968[14] mirrored the end of this period of liberal Catholicism. To leaf through the files of *Jubilee's* fifteen years of magazines is to excavate a lost era, an important segment of recent U.S. Catholicism that has vanished. As with any exercise in nostalgia, viewing the issues of *Jubilee* brings back a flood of memories. A lost society is rediscovered and illuminated. One asks, as the historian or archaeologist asks about some ancient society and that flourished and then disappeared without a trace, what happened? Where did all these people go? One also asks, what contribution, what lasting influence beside such artifacts as *Jubilee*, did Catholic liberals of this period have on U.S. Catholicism?

In Catholic high schools and colleges throughout the United States, in the homes of young Catholic couples, and in seminaries during the 1950s and early 1960s, the influence of *Jubilee* was paramount. It provided a subject of conversation and a point of view on Catholicism among the Catholic *avant garde*. I can remember how many of my classmates at the Universiy of San Francisco followed its *dicta*, how strongly it shaped our thinking abut the Church. George Devine (years later to become chairman of the religion department at Seton Hall University) was inspired to attend Sunday mass at the Russian Uniate church in San Francisco, Kevin Starr read omniverously the French Catholic theologians. Greg Calegari, a high school classmate who was in the seminary, encouraged his parents to follow the suggestions of *Jubilee* for a liturgical household.

I attempted after my marriage in 1962 to continue to live the all-pervasive Catholicism of *Jubilee*—and did, before the demands of work and raising a family and the ecclesiastical disintegration of the mid-1960s ended my commitment.

The *Jubilee* Catholic disappeared sometime during the mid- and late-1960s in a cataclysm that will be described later in this book. The movement of postwar liberal Catholicism has been variously assessed in the late 1960s and the 1970s as being "precious," a "hothouse flower," "too concerned with an aesthetic Catholicism," "not enough concerned with social justice," "too trusting of the ecclesiastical and political establishments of Church and State," and "too optimistic."

It is too soon to attempt an assessment of *Jubilee* Catholicism. When one reads the pages of *Commonweal* of the 1940s, 1950s, and early 1960s, and of *Jubilee* during its fifteen-year existence, one is struck by the changes in society in general which are reflected in U.S. Catholicism. These changes—changes in mood and aspirations brought about by the assassination of national leaders, by the enervating and divisive war in Vietnam, by violent eruptions in urban areas—gave rise to the harsh critique of postwar liberal Catholicism indicated above. In the light of these changes—and of concomitant changes in U.S. Catholicism—*Jubi-*

*lee* Catholicism does seem to have been a rare flower, perhaps something approximating *Yellow Book* decadence in England in the 1890s. When one chronicles the aborted institutions of *Jubilee* Catholicism, the collapse of its optimistic hopes for the future of U.S. Catholicism, the evaporation of its entire lifestyle, one is struck by its apparent failure. And when one views it in the light of large defections of priests and religious in the late 1960s and the 1970s, of what amounts to mass apostasy of Catholics during the same period, of the perspective of *Humanae Vitae* (the papal encyclical against artificial birth control), and of the evisceration of the institutional church in the United States, one can only conclude that *Jubilee* Catholicism was indeed a failure.

*Jubilee* Catholics have been accused by conservatives of having provided the agitation for the "radical" reforms—particularly those of the liturgy—that arose in the Church as a result of the Second Vatican Council. They have been accused by modern liberals of being too "churchy" and of being too establishment-oriented with regard both to the Church and to the United States Government. They have been accused of fiddling with Gregorian chant and playing with Eastern icons while racial injustice was rampant, while social and economic injustice were accepted facts of life on the national scene, and while an immoral war was beginning in the Far East.

As any historian knows, one cannot perceive or judge the past by the consciousness and precepts of the present. And most of the criticism of *Jubilee* Catholicism seems unjustified. The conservative accusation that *Jubilee* Catholics were responsible for a dreary vernacular liturgy and for what are viewed as other evils of postconciliar Catholicism is unfounded. In matters theological and liturgical, *Jubilee* Catholics were conservative. In fact, their liberalism was, paradoxically, a matter of a strong traditional bias in these matters. Also off the mark are the current liberal accusations that *Jubilee* Catholics somehow participated in racial injustice, in super-patriotic support for U.S. military intervention abroad, in accepting the status quo with regard to national social ills. *Jubilee* Catholics were people of their time—liberals in the vein of Adlai Stevenson or in the more pragmatic style of John F. Kennedy. Their concern for the racial problems of the United

States was expressed in the Catholic Interracial Council, not in street demonstrations. The papal social encyclicals and progressive social legislation were the *Jubilee* Catholics' form of dealing with social ills. With the exception of Dorothy Day and her followers in the Catholic Worker Movement, U.S. Catholics, including *Jubilee* Catholics, adhered to the conventional wisdom about the role of the United States in the containment of Communism throughout the world.

Although it is probably too early to judge the place of *Jubilee* Catholicism in the history of Catholicism in the United States, there is no doubt that this movement indicated a new sociological development among U.S. Catholics. It signaled the end of the era of "ghetto Catholicism," and the emergence of millions of descendents of Catholic immigrants into the mainstream of U.S. life. A strong identification with Catholicism remained in this emergence; and the greater affluence and education of these Catholics, influenced by the intellectual and artistic currents in the postwar United States, coupled with the lack of a Catholic intellectual heritage in U.S. Catholicism, caused them to become *Jubilee* Catholics.

In October, 1958, Pope Pius XII died. That austere pontiff, symbol of the majesty and durability of Roman Catholicism, was succeeded by the Patriarch of Venice, Angelo Cardinal Roncalli, who—shortly after he became Pope—announced that he would call an ecumenical council. The date for this council was set for the autumn of 1962. No one realized—at the election of Cardinal Roncalli as Pope John XXIII in 1958, or in his formal announcement of an ecumenical council in 1959, or at the time of the beginning of the council in 1962—what a momentous event this would be, and what volcanic effects the council would have.

Meanwhile, the attention of the United States—particularly Catholics—during 1959 and 1960 was focused on the efforts of a young senator from Massachusetts to win the Democratic nomination for the presidency, and after winning the nomination, on his drive to become elected despite the fact that he was a Catholic. John F. Kennedy, scion of a wealthy and active family, seemed the cynosure of the immigrant Catholic experience in the United States. His ancestors had emigrated from Ireland in the 1840s. They had fought bigotry and discrimination, but had prospered economically and been successful in politics. Nevertheless, many Americans, including most Catholics, felt after the defeat of Alfred E. Smith in 1928 that the presidency was beyond the reach of a Catholic. Kennedy, however, was unwilling to believe that his religion could prevent his election as president.

Tackling the religious issue head-on, Kennedy addressed the Greater Houston Ministerial Association on September 12, 1960. He not only made a masterful speech, but met questions from the floor in a forthright and open way that left his audience more than satisfied.

Kennedy's narrow victory on November 8, 1960, was due to a variety of factors. No one seems to be able to assess correctly whether he was ultimately helped or hurt by his religious beliefs. The great achievement of the election of John F. Kennedy as president of the United States was that the barrier against a Catholic's becoming president was erased, and the position of Catholics in the United States was thus elevated socially and politically. The campaign and the election had not changed any Catholic belief or practice, but they had increased greatly the public acceptance of Catholicism.

I can remember vividly the Kennedy campaign of 1959–1960, and the exuberant aftermath of his victory. This most sophisticated and glamorous young man, with his shimmering ideals, was not only a "knight in shining armor" politically, he was also a Catholic. No up-from-the-wards politician was John Kennedy, but someone who reinforced my pride in being Catholic.

And so, as the 1960s began, Catholics in the United States were joyfully optimistic. A Catholic had been elected president; and his charm, his attractive and interesting family, and his idealism, which he asked the nation to share with him, riveted the attention of Americans—and of the world.

In Rome, that other John, a short, stocky man of peasant origins who was in his late seventies, was rapidly showing that he did not mean to be a transitional, inactive pope. His smiling humility and approachability, his readiness to go anywhere, his friendliness, and his openness to non-Catholics augured well for the coming ecumenical council for the reform and renewal of the Church. He had proclaimed the *aggiornamento* as John Kennedy had announced the "new frontier."

For both the Catholic Church and for the United States, the early 1960s were to herald a new age.

# PART TWO

# *and now is the era of our discontent*

# 4/ The Second Vatican Council

*Ten years is not a long time in the history of an institution so
venerable as the Roman Catholic Church, and we are all
tempted arrogantly to overestimate the importance of the
recent past. Yet the last decade of the Church is not just an
arbitrary slice of history: it marks the period in which a
prodigious effort was made to assimilate the achievements of
Vatican II. It is this effort, with its successes, failures,
confusions, and ambiguities which has given the last decade a
certain unity.* Peter Hebblethwaite, The Runaway Church

The Graduate Theological Union at Berkeley, affiliated
with the University of California, consists of nine separate
schools of theology for Catholic religious orders and Protestant
denominations. Students from each are encouraged to take
courses from schools other than those of their own denominations or orders. Thus Sister Mary Ann Donovan of the Sisters of
Charity, attired modestly and attractively in "lay" clothes and
living in an apartment near the campus, teaches Lutheran, Con-
gregationalist, Unitarian, and Episcopalian—as well as Catholic—students a course entitled "The Emergence of Early Christianity." Father Kenan Osborne, head of the Franciscan School
of Theology, teaches the same heterogenous denominational
students in a course, "The Church and the Sacraments."

Standing before the students (who call him "Kenan") in sport
coat and tie, and discussing both the Church (into which term
he includes all Christian denominations) and the sacraments in
terms of post-Vatican II theological developments, Osborne

seems the embodiment of the effects of the last ecumenical council. Gone are the traditional brown Franciscan robes, the reverent appellation "Father," the doctrinaire assertion that the U.S. Catholic Church was synonymous with truth and salvation, and that the sacraments could only be discussed in Thomistic terms.

The election in 1958 of the jovial cardinal to succeed the awesome Pope Pius XII was a surprise to Catholics as well as non-Catholics. No change could be expected from the papacy of John XXIII, it was said, for he had been elected only because the conclave couldn't agree on another candidate. The new pope, who had spent virtually all his life as a papal diplomat, was thought to be a compromise choice who would not jolt the established order during the few years that remained of his life. He was just a transition choice, my friends and I told each other, who was put in because the cardinals couldn't agree on another candidate. He wouldn't do anything except try to preserve harmony.

But the world took immediately to this warm and friendly pope. His humanity was obvious to all. And soon to become obvious also was his intention of bringing up to date (*aggiornamento* was his word for it) the Roman Catholic Church by calling, in early 1959, for an ecumenical council—the first since the First Vatican Council of 1869–1870.

This council, called to convene in 1962, aroused a great deal of interest when announced. Very few observers, however, had any idea that it would become a revolutionary event. Most believed that after a great display of rhetorical debate and ceremonial pageantry nothing would be changed. Some believed that the council had been called to proclaim a dogma on the Blessed Virgin Mary. Probably none foresaw the vast energies that would be unleashed as a result of the three-year period during which bishops and theologians from throughout the world met in solemn council in St. Peter's Basilica.

For four hundred years before the Second Vatican Council, the Roman Catholic Church had been reeling from the onslaughts of disunity and the attacks of those who wished to destroy it. The Council of Trent had been called in the mid-sixteenth century in response to the Protestant Revolt; and during a period of twenty years this council hammered out an effective policy of Counter-Reformation that would influence the Church until the mid-twentieth century.

The shock of the Protestant Revolt was followed by the Enlightenment and the scientific revolution. The modern world had come into being; but for the Church the centuries since the Middle Ages had been productive only of error. In the minds of its leaders, the Church was a besieged bastion of Truth; and they did not hesitate to employ any means necessary to keep faithful Catholics from being corrupted by false teachings. Pope Pius IX contributed the *Syllabus of Errors* in 1864; and in 1910 Pope Pius X was to condemn the movement known as "Modernism." The expression "no salvation outside the Church" was a clear announcement of the Church's exclusivity.

On Thursday, October 11, 1962, Pope John XXIII addressed the council fathers on the official opening day of the twenty-first ecumenical council. After a few introductory remarks, the pope announced that he was tired of listening to the prophets of doom among his advisers, who maintained, he said, that the modern world is "full of prevarication and ruin."[1]

"Divine Providence is leading us to a new order of human relations," he declared. It was imperative for the Church "to bring herself up to date where required," in order to spread her message "to all men throughout the world." While the Church must "never depart from the sacred patrimony of truth received from the Fathers," she must "ever look to the present, to new conditions and new forms of life introduced into the modern world, which have opened new avenues to the Catholic apostolate."

The pope said that he had not called the council to discuss "one article or another of the fundamental doctrine of the Church . . . which is presumed to be well known and familiar to all; for this, a council was not necessary." No, said the pontiff; "the world expects a step forward toward doctrinal penetration and a formation of consciences." This must be "in conformity with authentic doctrine," of course, but it "should be studied and expounded through the methods of research and through the literary forms of modern thought." In other words, doctrine was to be made more intelligible to contemporaries in the light

of scholarship in biblical, theological, philosophical, and historical disciplines.

He next touched on a subject that is almost taboo in traditionalist Catholic theological circles, saying, "The substance of the
ancient doctrine of the *depositum fidei* is one thing; the way in
which it is expressed is another." That is, Catholic doctrine remains the same in substance, but the formulations of it vary and
are not regarded as unalterable ends in themselves. The task of
the council, he told the assembled prelates, was to find the best
formulas for our time, without being too hidebound or showing
too slavish a respect for those of a previous age. He further emphasized the pastoral (rather than the doctrinal) note by declaring, "Nowadays, the bride of Christ [the Church] prefers to
make use of the medicine of mercy rather than that of severity.
She considers that she meets the needs of the present day by
demonstrating the validity of her teaching rather than by condemnation."

Finally, the pope turned his attention to the problem of Christian unity. "The entire Christian family has not yet fully at-
tained the visible unity in truth" desired by Christ, he said, and
the Catholic Church "therefore considers it her duty to work actively so that there may be fulfilled the great mystery of that
unity." He said that the key to "the brotherly unity of all"—embracing not only Christians but "those who follow non-Christian religions"—is "the fullness of charity," or love. Thus Pope
John put his seal on the methods and goals of Catholic participation in the ecumenical, or worldwide, movement for reunion.

Deeds were the consquence of these words of the pontiff: for,
seated in St. Peter's as participants in the council, were observer
delegates from a myriad of non-Catholic churches—a participation unprecedented in the annals of Roman Catholicism.

The first session of the Second Vatican Council ended in December 1962. In June of 1963, Pope John XXIII died. His successor, Pope Paul VI, not only decided to reconvene the council at
an early date—the second session took place from September to
December 1963—but reaffirmed the council's purpose "to open
up new horizons in the Church, and to tap the fresh spring wa-

ter of the doctrine and grace of Christ our Lord and let it flow over the earth."

The three sessions of Vatican Council II—those held in 1963, 1964, and 1965—under Pope Paul VI were punctuated by that pontiff's innovative approaches to his office: notably, by his trip to the Holy Land and his meeting there with the Orthodox patriarch of Constantinople; his address to the United Nations in New York; and his trips to India and other countries.

The first *schema* to be debated by the council fathers in 1962 was that on the liturgy. Almost immediately, the debate centered on the universal use of Latin in the mass of the Western Church. Conservatives wished for retention of the Tridentine mass[2] said in Latin; progressives wished for part or all of the mass to be said in the vernacular. Debate on giving the laity communion with both bread and wine, on concelebration, and on whether the divine office could be chanted or recited in the vernacular[3] also marked the deliberation on the liturgy.

The conservatives lost this initial battle of the Second Vatican Council. The "Constitution on the Sacred Liturgy" was promulgated on December 4, 1963. (Practical implementation in the United States was to take place on the First Sunday of Advent in the following year.) A vernacularized, congregationally-participated liturgy was now on record as the clear will of the Church at its highest level of authority. Several years of liturgical experimentation would take place until the issuance in 1970 of Pope Paul VI's new *Odo Missae*, which was intended as signaling the end of these innovative experiments.

The council then discussed the *schema* entitled, "Sources of Revelation." Once more conservatives and progressives battled. The heated debate on this issue—basic, in a sense, to all else—focused on whether the Bible and tradition are two separate, virtually independent sources of divine revelation, or whether together they constitute a whole—two modes, written and unwritten, by which the Word of God comes down to us within the framework of the Church.

What sounds like a minor theological dispute was actually a

critical concept, influencing the ecumenical movement, Scripture studies, and other matters at the heart of Catholic doctrine. Xavier Rynne writes of the "Constitution on Divine Revelation," which, after much revision, was voted on and promulgated during the fourth session:

> There can be little doubt that the Constitution on Divine Revelation will be regarded as the most important document promulgated by the Council after the Constitution on the Church. Together with *Lumen Gentium*, it enshrined and consecrated the new biblical approach to theology which has become one of the hallmarks of Vatican II.[4]

The council's debate on the *schema* on "Modern Means of Communications" and the vote and promulgation of the revised *schema* need not detain us here. Most of the prelates failed to give the text or the debate on it much serious attention. Many thought that the subject merited some consideration, but was hardly worth the time of an ecumenical council. Some felt that it was so unworthy and compromising as to be voted down. Despite the severe criticism of some theologians and members of the media and an attempt by twenty-four bishops to have the *schema* voted down, it was passed.

The second session of the council debated the *schema* known as "The Church" (*De Ecclesia*), which many believe to have been the most important issue—and the most important document— to come out of the council. It was also one of the most intensely debated constitutions at the council. A list of the chapters contained in the "Constitution on the Church" gives an indication of its scope: I. The Mystery of the Church; II. On the people of God; III. The Hierarchical Structure of the Church: The Episcopate; IV. The Laity; V. The Universal Vocation to Holiness in the Church; VI. Religious; VII. The Eschatological Nature of the Pilgrim Church and Its Union with the Church in Heaven; VIII. The Blessed Virgin Mary, Mother of God, in the Mystery of Christ and the Church.

What emerges is a remarkable document that speaks of the "people of God," and states, "God gathered together as one all those who in faith look upon Jesus as the author of salvation and the source of unity and peace, and established them as the Church, that for each and all it may be the visible Sacrament of this saving unit."[5] The "Constitution on the Church" is a departure from what many had formerly considered to be the Church's doctrine that "there is no salvation outside the Church" (narrowly interpreted to mean in communion with Rome). "Those also can attain to salvation," says the constitution, "who through no fault of their own do not know the Gospel of Christ of His Church, yet sincerely seek God and moved by grace strive by their deeds to do His will as it is known to them through the dictates of conscience."[6]

As if the controversy on the nature of the Church were not enough for the second session, the council also at this time debated the *schema* "Ecumenism." The final decree was promulgated on November 21, 1964. One of the principles most vigorously debated between conservatives and liberals concerned the reasons for disunity among Christian churches. The conservatives' position that no blame could be attached to the Roman Catholic Church at any time was dashed: the *Decree on Ecumenism* proclaimed, ". . . In subsequent centuries [following the apostolic beginnings of Christianity] much more serious dissensions made their appearance and quite large communities came to be separated from full communion with the Catholic Church—for which, often enough, men of both sides were to blame."[7]

A call to Catholics to seek unity through the ecumenical movement, which had been officially frowned upon previous to the council, was stated in the following manner:

> Today, in many parts of the world, under the inspiring grace of the Holy Spirit, many efforts are being made in prayer, word and action to attain that fullness of unity which Jesus Christ desires. The sacred council exhorts all the Catholic faithful to recognize the signs of the times and to take an active and intelligent part in the work of ecumenism.
>
> The term "ecumenical movement" indicates the initiatives and activities planned and undertaken, according to the various

needs of the Church and as opportunities offer, to promote Christian unity.[8]

The remainder of the *Decree on Ecumenism* deals with the Christian churches separated from Roman Catholicism. These are divided into the Eastern churches (Orthodox) and the separated churches and ecclesial communities in the West (Protestant). The former, states the decree, are in a special position to Roman Catholicism—what had been called "schismatic," as opposed to the "heretical" relationship of the Protestant churches.

Such men as the German Jesuit Cardinal Bea and a number of prelates from the United States strongly favored a statement on the Jews. Such a statement, claimed those who proposed it, would be a clear exposition that the Catholic Church does not consider Jews to be "Christ killers." This announcement would disarm those in the future who would use the crucifixion of Christ as a basis for anti-Semitism. However, the issuance of such a statement aroused controversy—much of it from council fathers from Arab states, who feared that such a decree would have political repercussions in their countries.

The decree was sent back for redrafting, and emerged as part of the *Declaration on the Relation of the Church to Non-Christian Religions*. Thus, the declaration mentions Hindus and Buddhists, and covers more extensively Moslems and Jews. As with the *Decree on Ecumenism*, the council urged contacts with these religious groups:

> The Church, therefore, exhorts her sons, that through dialogue and collaboration with the followers of other religions, carried out with prudence and love and in witness to the Christian faith and life, they recognize, preserve and promote the good things, spiritual and moral, as well as the socio-cultural values found among these men.[9]

Yet another controversy swirled around the *Declaration on Religious Liberty*. For many years it had been the Church's position that a "perfect society" is one where the spiritual and the secular realms are "as one." In short, the ideal was that merger of Church and State that had come about in the early fourth century, when Constantine had decreed Christianity an authorized religion of the Roman Empire. This ideal was the theoretical construct of the political and religious experience of the Middle Ages.

However, the modern world offered a different reality. Many countries persecuted the Catholic Church; others allowed it to exist without any special privileges. In the distinctive, pluralistic political framework of the United States, Catholicism was able to flourish without a basis as a state church and along with numerous other religious bodies. Given what seemed to be the official stance of Catholicism, however, many individuals claimed that if the Catholic Church ever achieved a majority of the population in the United States, the basic constitutional liberty of freedom of religion would be subverted. It was probably no coincidence that the leading theologian of religious freedom at this time was a U.S. Jesuit, the late John Courtney Murray. Murray's carefully worked out theology of religious freedom was spurned by conservatives, and he found himself under an official cloud of censure. No invitation came to this eminent theologian to attend the Second Vatican Council; and it was not until the second session that he was able to appear—as a personal theologian of Cardinal Spellman. And it was only then that his theological theories began to prevail and to be incorporated into the official teaching of the Church.

The initial statement of the *Declaration on Religious Liberty* sets forth the tone of the document:

> A sense of the dignity of the human person has been impressing itself more and more deeply on the consciousness of contemporary man, and the demand is increasingly made that men should act on their own judgment, enjoying and making use of a responsible freedom, not coercion but motivated by a sense of duty. The demand is likewise made that constitutional limits should be set to the powers of government, in order that there may be no encroachment on the rightful freedom of the person and of associations.[10]

The declaration affirms that the "one true religion subsists in the Catholic and Apostolic Church" and that it is "the moral duty of men (to seek) the true religion and . . . the one Church of Christ." However, the declaration states:

> This Vatican Council declares that the human person has a right to religious freedom. This freedom means that all men are to be immune from coercion on the part of individuals or of social groups and of any human power, in such wise that no one is to be forced to act in a manner contrary to his own beliefs, whether privately or publicly, whether alone or in association with others, within due limits.
>
> The council further declares that the right to religious freedom has its foundation in the very dignity of the human person as this dignity is known through the revealed word of God and by reason itself. This right of the human person to religious freedom is to be recognized in the constitutional law whereby society is governed and thus it is to become a civil right.[11]

Thus, the long tradition of the Church in using the secular power to "stamp out error" came to an end. The *Declaration on Religious Liberty*, rarely thought about today, was one of the most significant achievements of the Second Vatican Council.

In the light of events in postconciliar Catholicism, three other decrees should also be looked at: on the life and ministries of priests, on the appropriate renewal of the religious life, and on priestly formation. All three decrees were essentially conservative documents: most of what was said in them was already part of the common teaching of the Church. However, what may have seemed at the time of the council innocuous provisions for priestly and religious renewal would, in the years after Vatican Council II, provide the basis for a revolution.

It must be remembered that the century following the issuance of the *Syllabus of Errors* by Pius IX was a period of great conservatism in the Church. Parish curates were little more than peons under the all-powerful authority of the pastor. All priests in a diocese were subject to the limitless authority of the bishop. This authoritarian structure was also characteristic of the religious orders. Theological training in seminaries rarely rose above the memorization of propositions in jejune manuals. Accretions of customs and regulations from earlier eras became embedded as part of the everyday life of religious orders. For example, religious garb, for most religious orders, was the dress that had been in use many centuries before when the orders were founded. Such garments and regulations, while often colorful (as, for example, the distinctive, floppy white headgear of the Sisters of Charity), were thought by many to be outmoded and inconvenient by the second half of the twentieth century.

The three decrees—in the spirit of *aggiornamento*—called for an examination of seminary training, of the role of priests, and of religious life, with a view to renewing and updating these aspects of the Church. The vague provisions of the decrees that seemed most radical were that: (1) the seminary should be modernized (*Decree on Priestly Formation*); (2) the bishop should listen to and consult with his priests, and that he should formally accomplish this by establishing a priests' senate or similar representative body (*Decree on the Life and Ministries of Priests*); and (3) religious orders should reexamine the rules, constitutions, customs, and structures under which they are governed and adapt them to the needs of contemporary society (*Decree on the Appropriate Renewal of the Religious Life*). In this latter decree, the superiors of religious orders were advised to allow all members of the order to involve themselves in the process of renewal and to allow "prudent experimentation." Religious habits were specifically mentioned: they should be modest and simple, said the decree, and should meet the requirements of health and be suited to the situations and services required by those who wear them.

These provisions did not seem controversial or radical at the time they were drafted, voted upon favorably, and promulgated. Probably no council father could have foreseen the storms that would accompany implementation of the decrees.

The last document of the Second Vatican Council that we will discuss in this chapter is the *Decree on the Apostolate of the Laity*. Many of the more progressive council fathers thought it a weak document and felt, despite its laudatory terms for the laity, that it was partonizing and depicted the laity as appendages of the clergy and hierarchy. Nevertheless, this long document calls for both a spirituality of laypersons and a lay apostolate, the sharing of the work of spreading the Gospel. The decree goes into greater detail than most of the council documents in discussing the various apostolates open to the laity and the training necessary for them.

Once again, as with the decrees on priestly training and ministry and on renewal of the religious life, the consequences of this decree were not foreseen at the time of Vatican Council II.

Even after the decade-and-a-half that has elapsed since the termination of the Second Vatican Council in 1965, any assessment of its effects is difficult. The council was a great public relations success: the media covered it extensively, and on the whole quite favorably. Hundreds of books tumbled off the presses, describing, critiquing, and analyzing the proceedings. (There was even one massive volume of almost seven hundred pages that described the rather undistinguished contribution of U.S. prelates at the council.) Catholics and non-Catholics alike contributed to this analysis in hundreds of books and thousands of articles. And most evaluations have praised the Second Vatican Council. It has been called "the council that put a 'period' to the scholastic age of the Church," "a fundamental reappraisal of Catholicism," "the most significant event in Christianity since the Reformation," and "the end of Counter-Reformation Catholicism." From blow-by-blow accounts of the sessions of Vatican Council II to sophisticated theological commentaries on its decrees, the literature on the proceedings has been vast. But even with all of this available literature, any definitive assessment is premature.

There is no doubt that the council was a watershed experience for Catholicism—and perhaps for all Christianity—in modern times. There is no doubt that the council took seriously and sincerely Pope John's call for *aggiornamento* (Pope Paul preferred the word *rinnovamento,* renewal). And there is no doubt that the council had a major impact on the future of Catholicism. Perhaps one of the most balanced appraisals came from the pen of the pseudonymous Xavier Rynne:

> It has become something of a commonplace to say of the Council, "Nothing has changed, even though things will never be the

same again." Taking the work of the Council as a whole and considering it from a purely superficial point of view, it is not difficult to make out that there have been few radical changes and to put the stress on continuity. Almost every conciliar statement has its counterpart in the theological literature of the recent past (though what the shortsighted fail to point out is that many of these statements occur in the writings of those formerly considered "heretics"). Though all the documents bear the mark of compromise, when the successive versions of the documents are placed side by side one can . . . see what tremendous strides have been made.

What the Council has really done is to lay the groundwork for a thorough "reappraisal" of Catholicism. . . . More important than the documents themselves, the Council has consecrated a new spirit destined in the course of time to remake the face of Catholicism. More important than the specific provisions of this or that decree, are the truly revolutionary, biblically-oriented principles found scattered throughout the Council's work, which in time will bring about the necessary transformation and lead ultimately to the desired goal of reunion."[12]

Rynne's optimism, from his perspective in 1966, may today seem unwarranted. The fissures in the Church's organization and the tensions in Catholicism would become more visible in the future; unprecedented defections of priests and religious from their ministries and vows and what has amounted to mass apostasy—to use an old-fashioned word—among the laity had not yet dispelled the postconciliar euphoria; the "indifferentism" that conservatives at the council had predicted (and for which sentiments of doom they were scorned and derided) had not yet become a reality.

The Second Vatican Council has been blamed by many for the tumult in Catholicism that followed in its wake: for a barren liturgy; for priests and religious abandoning their vocations; for many Catholics, particularly younger ones, ceasing to become practicing Catholics; for an increasingly speculative theology that received great attention in the media and seemingly called into question the most fundamental truths of Catholicism. The fact that following Vatican Council II a broad cross section of Catholics have forged an actual, if not a technical, schism, spearheaded by Archbishop Marcel Lefebvre; that many Catholics no longer go to mass and Communion and have only the vaguest sense of being Catholic; and that the decline of those entering seminaries and novitiates has threatened the ability of the Church to perform its traditional pastoral role all seem to give credence to a cause and effect chain of events reverting to the council.

No such conclusion is warranted at this time. And no analysis of the council's effects on Catholicism is yet possible. Those who ascribe to Vatican Council II the cause for the ferment, the volcanic eruptions, the seeming irrelevance in postconciliar Catholicism seem to be engaging in the classic fallacy of logic, *post hoc, ergo propter hoc* (it happened after it, therefore it happened because of it). Also fallacious seems to be the conclusion of sociologist Andrew Greeley, who declares that Catholics did not object to the work of the council, and that the "ills" of contemporary Catholicism can be traced to the issuance of Pope Paul VI's encyclical against artificial birth control, *Humanae Vitae*, in 1968.[13] Such conclusions of cause and effect miss the point in attempting to explain the extraordinary events in Catholicism in the decade and a half following Vatican Council II.

Any *bona fide* assessment of the council's effects must await the passage of time and the analytical tools of the various disciplines of the social sciences. For an analysis of the impact of the Second Vatican Council on Catholicism is not only a matter of theological commentary: it is also very much a matter for historical, sociological, anthropological, and psychological inquiry. It is not only a matter of what the council did or did not do from a strictly theological viewpoint: it is also a matter of what millions of Catholics throughout the world, individually and collectively, *perceived* it doing or not doing. The "spirit of Vatican II" became a shibboleth capable of diverse interpretation.

The "spirit of Vatican II," according to Dr. James Hitchcock,[14] was largely the figment of the imagination of those who wished to "throw off the traces" of historical Catholicism, although most of the radical Catholics of the postconciliar period had not bothered to read the conciliar documents. Whether that was or was not the case, these radical Catholics appealed for a Catholicism beyond the promulgated documents—once again, the vague and undefined "spirit of Vatican II."

Further, the impact of the Second Vatican Council must be viewed and assessed within the context of the times—the 1960s and 1970s. The decade of the 1960s began with great optimism. For Catholics in the United States the beginning of the 1960s was a particular time for rejoicing. The pope—John XXIII—who had been elected two years before was beloved by all and had called for an ecumenical council. The president—John F. Kennedy—was the first Catholic ever elected president of the United States, and with his attractive family and energetic entourage, he was creating a "Camelot" in Washington. The theological optimism of Teilhard de Chardin was the appropriate gospel for the new administration; and it is probably no coincidence that the principal spokesman in the administration for efficiently applied technology as a solution for most of the world's evils, Robert McNamara, read and admired Teilhard de Chardin.

The assassination of John F. Kennedy in late 1963 put an end to the idealistic period his style had engendered in national politics. The realization that in the United States there still existed widespread poverty, hunger, unemployment, and other ills gave rise to the concept of "the Great Society" by Kennedy's successor, Lyndon B. Johnson. As the Second Vatican Council ended in late 1965, there was almost a sense of euphoria about how its effects would revitalize the Church; and similarly, throughout the United States, there was exuberant optimism about vast new programs to battle poverty and about legislation and court decisions to end racial discrimination. No one seemed to notice that the United States in 1965 had decided to commit vast resources to the persistent war in Vietnam. After all, most thought, how can a few guerrillas and the army of a pathetically small nation, North Vietnam, withstand the might of the United States?

Then something happened. With a rapidity that seems startling even today, the situation deteriorated. The comparatively gentle probings of Selma and that popular oracle of a "new age," *The Secular City*, gave way to harsh violence in the inner cities of urban areas throughout the United States, and on college and university campuses throughout the country.

Ending the war in Vietnam proved as elusive as ending poverty and social injustice in the United States. The optimism of the early 1960s turned into harsh disillusionment during the second half of the decade. The backlash was terrifying: an almost revolutionary fervor in defying the system that had failed, that had been immoral, and that had been unable to deliver on its promises. Every institution came under attack—principally by the most visible rebels during this period, the young.

The election of Richard M. Nixon as president in 1968 and the persistence of the enervating conflict in Vietnam seemed to intensify the protest in the United States as the decade drew to a close. The cessation of the war and the subsequent resignation of President Nixon in the aftermath of the Watergate scandals provided a national catharsis. The decade of tumult came to an end. The volcanic energies of protest ebbed. The ferment of radical change burned out. The nation sought tranquility.

It was in this atmosphere that U.S. Catholicism sought to implement the Second Vatican Council; and no analysis of U.S. Catholicism in the aftermath of the council can be undertaken without considering the social and political factors described above. It is to the postconciliar Church in the United States that we now turn our attention.

# 5/ And the Walls Came Tumbling Down

In the beginning, around 1964, the turmoil that was to shake the Church was like a small cloud on the horizon. Within two or three years storm clouds filled the sky. And by the mid-1970s the U.S. Catholic Church was a tempest-tossed institution in total disarray.

Even though these events in U.S. Catholicism occurred comparatively recently, they have today receded into dim memory. The relative calm of the past few years has tended to obscure the renewal-turned-into-revolution that racked U.S. Catholicism during the decade following the Second Vatican Council. In earlier times, it would have been unthinkable that the docile U.S. Catholic Church, with its long traditions of respect for its bishops and priests, love for its nuns, acceptance of the Church's teachings, obedience to its rules, and huge numbers in attendance at mass, would become convulsed for a decade with attacks on the pope, bishop-baiting, and an unprecedented exodus of priests, brothers, and nuns from their vocations. Theological statements were issued that formerly would have branded their authors as heretics; and priests and religious were arrested for their protests against racial and social injustice and U.S. involvement in Vietnam.

It was as if a long-capped volcano had erupted. The lives of individual Catholics were radically changed. The U.S. Catholic Church was split into factions hostile to each other. The "people of God," so movingly proclaimed at the Second Vatican Council, became a squabbling mass of individuals eager to dismantle the

U.S. Catholic Church of the past—a modern version of the biblical story of the Tower of Babel. Father Philip Berrigan, a Catholic priest at the forefront of the anti-Vietnam war protest movement, called the institutional Catholic Church "a whore." A pastor in California revealed that he had been secretly married for many years, and wrote for an eager press an article entitled, "I Was a Married Priest." An unprecedented numbers of U.S. Catholics ceased going to mass each Sunday—many no longer even identifying themselves nominally as "Catholic." The U.S. Catholic school system, which had once been the glory of the U.S. Church, built up with great sacrifice over the years with small contributions from poor immigrants, was almost dismantled.

What happened? What caused these convulsions? What transpired to transform the pious, preconciliar U.S. Catholic Church into the strife-torn, disintegrating institution of the late 1960s and early 1970s? Any analysis of this period should begin with a selective recapitulation of the events in U.S. Catholicism from 1964 to 1975. And such a recapitulation should be viewed against the background of U.S. society during that decade. This was a United States which had gone from the Camelot idealism of the Kennedy years to the massive efforts of the Johnson administration to end poverty in the United States, to call an end to racial injustice, and to galvanize the vast resources of the country to stop urban blight. By the mid-1960s, however, it was becoming evident that these tasks, so hopefully begun, were not producing "the great society" that their advocates had proclaimed. The ensuing frustration created a mounting crescendo of criticism, and the expanding conflict in Vietnam compounded both the frustration and the criticism. The politics of violence were everywhere—it was a decade of dissent. An entire generation rebelled against authority. Cities erupted. Burning of entire sections of U.S. cities, looting, and full-scale battles with police and National Guard brought the plight of the urban disenfranchised to the attention of the nation. Colleges and universities became the crucibles of violent dissent. Protestors poured blood on draft records and then burned them. Traditional values were set aside—and often denounced—as the would-be makers of a new order blamed the ills of society on the established institutions—church, state, corporations, academia.

This dissent was not limited to the few. A collective feeling of guilt about having allowed these ills to fester led many to espouse the causes of the radical dissenters. Leonard Bernstein gave a breakfast for the Black Panthers. J. Sinclair Armstrong, executive vice president of the U.S. Trust Company of New York and former assistant secretary of the Navy under Eisenhower, marched in antiwar protests.

It is not surprising, in retrospect, that U.S. Catholicism should have participated in the dissent of the 1960s, that it should not only have become involved in the burning issues of social and racial injustice and the war in Vietnam, but in comparable issues pertaining to the Church itself. After all, did not the reforms slated for secular society—voting rights for blacks, an end to poverty, equal opportunity for all, sharing of decision-making power—have their religious counterpart in the reforms decreed and promised in the Second Vatican Council?

Still another phenomenon in U.S. Catholicism would help to cause the tumultuous events of the decade following the close of the Second Vatican Council: political awareness. The almost separatist and other-worldly aspects of the U.S. Church could not exist forever. The election of John F. Kennedy and the convening of the Second Vatican Council had combined to usher U.S. Catholics into the mainstream of American society. The economic and social advances of Catholics—and the gradual disappearance of the immigrant aspects of the U.S. Church—had ended the beleagured "ghetto mentality" of most Catholics in the years following the Second World War. Catholics had been "super-patriots" because that proved that they could be both fervently Catholic and loyally American: now they felt justified in burning draft files. Catholics were "a people apart," the traditional response of the U.S. Catholic Church to living in a pluralistic—and often hostile—society: now was the time to end this separatism. Did not the Council mandate an ecumenical spirit? And didn't the Gospels urge Christians to be witnesses? What better way to do so than to protest the moral outrages of the war in Vietnam, the discrimination against blacks, the dehumanizing poverty in the cities?

The world of Catholic separatism was not just a phenomenon of the Catholic laity, which sent its children to separate schools and received medical care in Catholic hospitals. It was most evident in the lives of the thousands of seminarians, priests, brothers, and nuns who had been called by God to the sacerdotal or religious life. A seminary on a remote Maryland farm no longer seemed in keeping with the spirit of the times for Jesuits studying theology. Sell the place, then, move to the West Side of Manhattan, and live in apartment houses just like any other students. Contacts of seminarians with the outside world had hitherto been limited by rigid rules. Instead, why not give each seminarian his own checkbook, allow women into the buildings where they lived, and let these students participate in antiwar demonstrations, minister to the needs of the poor Puerto Ricans in Harlem, and permit them to go to movies, rock concerts, and plays whenever they wished? If such policies resulted in chaos in the seminary and in seminarians abandoning their vocations to marry, well, that was the price you paid for freedom. And better that they should leave now, than be unhappy as priests.[1]

Had nuns been too cloistered; strangely dressed madonnas who spent their time toiling in schools and hospitals? Then let them come out into the world, dress like other women, sit in coffee houses and have rap sessions with seminarians and priests, and participate in the exciting events going on in society. It was "un-Christian" to wear those voluminous folds of black material, to shave one's head, to live in total obedience to one's superior and to the outdated rules of one's order. And teaching kindergarten at St. Philomena's Grammar School or emptying bedpans at Our Lady of Mercy Hospital wasn't what Christ had intended for the religious life. Normal human relationships including those with men, peace marches, and demonstrations against the reactionary episcopate—these were more in accordance with His wishes.

U.S. Catholicism has not wanted for its explanations of the disasters that overtook it during the decade following the Second Vatican Council. The conservatives in the polarized Church of this period blamed the changes brought about by the council and the radical theology that began to be widely discussed in its wake. The liberals blamed the hierarchy and the Roman curia for foot-dragging in implementing conciliar-inspired renewal of Catholicism.

Father Andrew Greeley and his associates, in *Catholic Schools in a Declining Church*, offer a compendium of the reasons for the decline in U.S. Catholicism; and based on their sociological researches, they reject the first three models in favor of the fourth. Their first reason is the "it would have happened anyway" model. "According to this view," they write, "the demographic and educational changes that have taken place in American Catholicism since the end of the Second World War have weakened both the intellectual and organizational structures of the immigrant church as well as the loyalty of Catholics to that church."[2] The second reason the sociologists give is the "reaction against the Council" model, and they write:

> "They [proponents of this argument] contend that the Catholic population has been "turned off" by the changes in the Church in the last ten years. However favorable their initial reaction might have been to the Second Vatican Council, the endless innovations since its conclusion have annoyed and angered the ordinary Catholic, who has reacted to the unwelcome changes by increasingly disaffiliating himself from the Church.[3]

They discuss the third possible reason—the "meat on Friday" model—as follows:

> From this viewpoint the fundamental mistake of Catholic leadership in the last decade was to permit change at all. Once one part of the tightly integrated structure of immigrant Catholicism was called into question, then everything could be questioned. Once it became legitimate to eat meat on Friday, one could doubt the authority of the pope, practice birth control, leave the priesthood and get married, or, indeed, do anything else one wanted to.[4]

Finally, we come to the fourth reason—the birth control-encyclical model—and that which the authors feel is the underlying reason for the deterioration of U.S. Catholicism. They write:

> Another explanation would exonerate the Vatican Council from responsibility, arguing that the Council was a successful enterprise in reform which was frustrated in its application by the conspiratorial activities of the Roman Curia after its adjournment, by the vacillating administration of Paul VI, and , especially, by the first birth control encyclical, *Humanae Vitae*, issued in 1967 [sic] and reaffirming the traditional Catholic birth-control teachings despite widespread expectations to the contrary. After the excitement of the Second Vatican Council, it is argued, there was a tremendous euphoria and expectation for change in the Church. It was taken for granted by both the Catholic elite and the Catholic masses that many of the more rigid, restrictive Catholic practices would be modified. Pope John had established a commission for reviewing the birth control issue. . . . as soon as birth control appeared to become a discussable issue, it automatically ceased to enjoy the status of an immutable doctrine. If one could discuss change, change itself was no longer an *a priori* impossibility. The reaffirmation of the birth control teaching in 1968, it is claimed, had a profoundly disillusioning effect on Catholic clergy, lay elite, and Catholic masses. It created a distaste for and alienation from the ecclesiastical institution.[5]

Given the amount of press coverage of the birth control issue and the proclamation of the encyclical, considering that the pope had overturned the findings of the papal commission selected to review this subject, and taking into account the body of theological opinion contrary to the pope's encyclical and the repudiation of it by the Catholic laity and the majority of priests, it is not surprising that those who responded to the authors' questionnaire reproduced in *Catholic Schools in a Declining Church* would have fastened on the very specific issue of the birth control prohibition as the symbol of their disaffection with the Church.

I believe, however, that such an analysis is too simplistic. There is abundant evidence that U.S. Catholicism was in disarray before the pope issued *Humanae Vitae*. What happened in

U.S. Catholicism, beginning during the last year of the Second Vatican Council, is dramatically chronicled in the pages of the weekly newspaper, the *National Catholic Reporter*, which began publication in October 1964. To read its fifteen years of reportage is to study the external events then taking place as well as the commentary and opinion about an institution "coming apart at the seams." Avowedly representing the liberal segment of U.S. Catholicism and an ecumenical spirit (the publication had both a Protestant and a Jew among its regular columnists), the *National Catholic Reporter* opened its pages to a broad spectrum of Catholic opinion: most notably, conservatives Garry Wills and Dr. James Hitchcock, and liberal John Leo. The liberal/conservative polarity in U.S. Catholicism, present for some decades, was intensified during the Second Vatican Council and its aftermath; and the "Letters to the Editors" and "Personal Opinion" sections of the *National Catholic Reporter* during this period were filled with the passionate invective that individuals representing each group hurled at each other. In a more urbane—even friendly— way, conservative columnist Garry Wills and liberal columnist John Leo dueled weekly with their pens.

The following selective sampling of the *National Catholic Reporter's* reportage is meant to catalyze an "act of memory," a resurrection of those events which almost fifty million U.S. Catholics—Catholics of all political and social shades, persuasions, and involvements—participated in or observed from the mid-1960s to the mid-1970s. And if a Catholic did not read about these events in the *National Catholic Reporter*, he or she could read about most of them in the daily press and in the national newsmagazines.

These writings represented a dramatic departure from the gentle essays on liturgical renewal, lay participation, and the need for Catholic social action, marked by their loyalty to the papacy and the hierarchy, that appeared in progressive Catholic publications from the 1930s to the early 1960s. The lectures, writings, and events of the decade following the Second Vatican Council were clearly revolutionary—a radical departure from the mild dissent of previous years. And for U.S. Catholicism—known for its docility toward ecclesiastical authority, for its high percentage of sacramental and devotional participation, and for its exalted image of pope, bishops, priests, nuns, and brothers—the events that took place from the mid-1960s to the mid-1970s were a shock, a series of bewildering changes that produced confusion and apathy and a widespread turning away from the traditional practice of Catholicism.

The very earliest issues of the *National Catholic Reporter* in 1964 discussed the question of the growing involvement of priests and religious in social justice issues. Are such issues within the proper scope of the ministry of priests and religious? It was to be a question that would haunt U.S. Catholicism for many years to come, and one that would soon balloon in scope.

In late 1964 and throughout 1965, nuns began to change their mode of dress. It is difficult today to remember how attention-getting these changes were when they first began to occur. The pages of the *National Catholic Reporter*—and the secular press as well—were filled with stories and photographs of the new designs in habits. As the ample folds of material were reduced, as hems were lifted from the floor to below the knees, as the all-encompassing headgear became a simple veil, the creations of Christian Dior, Yves St. Laurent, and Rudi Gernreich were shoved off the news pages in order that the new fashions of nuns might be presented.

But the changes of dress among nuns were only part of the self-analysis that began at this time. The Second Vatican Council had charged religious orders with renewal and a greater assimilation into contemporary life. This charge set in motion an examination of every aspect of the religious institutes of these orders: authority, obedience, how one should structure one's day, traditional apostolates, how one should live in community. Needless to say, the greater freedom to individuals mandated as a result of this self-analysis, the changes brought about by it, and the attraction of social justice causes that marked this period caused many nuns to examine not only the institute and way of life of their orders, but their own vocations.

Another change also began to be discernible at this time. Although U.S. Catholicism had always contained elements of the secular, it was paid greater homage beginning in the mid-1960s.[6]

For example, Sister Mary Corita, I.H.M., who might have been called "the drawing nun," used the popular technique of graphic art to produce a poster of a tomato with the accompanying legend, "Mary Mother is the juiciest tomato of them all."[7]

The year 1965, the last session of the council, was filled with ferment. Ecumenical contacts at the parish level became frequent. Divesting of the symbols of wealth to aid the poor became popular: Pope Paul VI donated his tiara to Cardinal Spellman to raise money for the poor, and nuns sold their rings, symbols of their "wedding" to Christ, for the same purpose. Seminaries began a long process of modernizing their curricula and their way of life.

This was the year of beginning Catholic involvement in social and racial injustice protest and in demonstrations against the conflict in Vietnam. A priest of the Archdiocese of Los Angeles, William Du Bay, called the archbishop, James Cardinal McIntyre, a racist, thus beginning a sharp feud between the two men and their respective followers. Du Bay would later attempt to form a union of priests. Daniel and Philip Berrigan, brothers and priests, began their protest of U.S. involvement in Vietnam. Among the marchers that year to Selma, Alabama, were numerous priests and nuns. And in June, Sisters Jane, Edwardine, Pauline, Bridget, Gloria, and Andrea were arrested, hauled off in a police van, and jailed after demonstrating against the purported racist policies of Chicago superintendent of schools Benjamin C. Willis.[8] Two weeks later a photograph in the *National Catholic Reporter* showed Father William Hogan of St. Martin's Church being carried off by two policemen after participating in another demonstration against Mr. Willis.[9] In 1965, Father James Groppi of Milwaukee began his militant career espousing the rights of blacks and the poor; David J. Miller and five others from the Catholic Worker movement were arrested for burning their draft cards; and another Catholic Worker movement member, Roger La Porte, immolated himself and died in protest against the Vietnam war.

Even as the Second Vatican Council ended, the U.S. Catholic Church was beset by problems and controversies. A substantial drop in priestly vocations and a large increase in seminarians leaving were noted by the *National Catholic Reporter*.[10] Father Gommar De Pauw began the Catholic Traditionalist Movement.[11] Priestly celibacy, contraception, and liturgical renewal became hotly debated topics. While Catholic prelates and clergy were preaching renewal, theologians at Emory University in Atlanta were proclaiming "the death of God."

Reaction against this ferment was immediate. The *National Catholic Reporter*, soon after it commenced publication, was criticized for its hostile attitude toward the hierarchy and for its anti-Vietnam war stance. The pope and numerous U.S. bishops scored the rising chorus of criticism of the Church. Daniel Berrigan, S.J., was silenced and exiled to Latin America.[12] St. John's University, a Catholic university in New York, fired twenty-four teachers, initiating a controversy that almost destroyed the institution.[13] Several seminarians were expelled from St. John's Seminary in Boston because they picketed Cardinal Cushing.[14]

There began in 1966 a new phenomenon—the public avowal of priests and nuns leaving their vocations and marrying. For the next few years, the pages of the *National Catholic Reporter* resembled the social columns of the secular press. In June 1966 it reported the marriage of Jesuit priest Lawrence J. Cross, age forty-seven, and twenty-seven-year-old Joan Rensud. They were married by Father Thomas J. Blackburn, S.J., of the University of Detroit.[15] Such an event was unprecedented in the annals of the Church. In the past, a priest who wished to leave the priesthood did so as quietly as possible: lapsed priests were anathema to the Catholic community. An ex-priest who married was doubly excoriated. And to have Blackburn, a priest "in good standing," officiate at the marriage of such an excommunicated renegade as Cross added a new dimension to this novelty.

It was not to be a novelty for long. A torrent of priests and nuns began to depart from their vocations—most of them to marry, and many to marry each other. The Church responded by "laicizing" (dispensing from priestly and religious vows and returning to lay status) virtually all those who sought this dispensation. (Thus was set up the not-illogical query of Catholic laity: If a priest can be dispensed from a supposedly perpetual vow, why can't divorced Catholics be dispensed from marriage vows?)

The controversies and strife expanded. The physical buildings and institutions of the Church were described as "wasteful," not conducive to prayer or worship, a symbol of the triumphal Church of the past. Nuns left their convents to live in apartments. But it was Catholic schools that came under the most sustained criticism: they were increasingly considered unnecessary and divisive; and they were accused of engendering separatism and lack of social concern among their students. Furthermore, the schools were expensive; especially with the exodus of the nuns, who had provided cheap teaching labor. It was this factor of growing expense, probably coupled with the desire of bishops and priests to show how "modern" they were, that caused a virtual cessation of building Catholic schools, and the closing of many existing schools.[16] Cyril D. Tyson, a black, urged U.S. Catholics to sell their schools to further a "slumless America."[17]

Shock waves were felt throughout Great Britain and the United States when British priest-theologian Charles Davis left both the priesthood and the Catholic Church.[18] Shortly thereafter, Sister Jacqueline Grennan, a Sister of Loretto, president of Webster College (which she secularized), and an intimate of Washington politicians during the Kennedy administration, announced that she would no longer be a nun.[19]

By 1967 the controversies over "the spirit of the Second Vatican Council," over what constituted reform and renewal of Catholicism, had rent the Church asunder. Archbishop Krol of Philadelphia suspended a twenty-six-year-old priest for minor infractions of the liturgical code.[20] There were demonstrations against Cardinal Spellman in St. Patrick's Cathedral in New York. Priests' senates came into being in late 1966 and early 1967. Rome scotched Jesuit plans to have Jesuit seminarians volunteer for VISTA. The bishops in Missouri stopped a convention of seminarians of the Cardinal Glennon Seminary. The unrest growing on college and university campuses did not spare Catholic institutions of higher learning. On April 26, 1967, two headlines in the *National Catholic Reporter* read: "Faculty, students close Catholic U. in firing protest" (of Father Charles Curran, a moral theologian) and "Students defy Boston College, hold lecture on birth control."[21]

Father James Kavanaugh grabbed national headlines for his

outspoken criticism of the Church and for his departure from the priesthood and his subsequent marriage. His article for the *Saturday Evening Post,* "I Am a Priest. I Want to Get Married," and his book, *A Modern Priest Looks at His Outdated Church,* are sensational barrages against the Church.

The year 1967 saw the founding of the National Association of Laymen and the publication of the Dutch catechism, which became the "bible" of liberal Catholics in the United States. In the same year, the U.S. bishops suppressed experimental parishes, setting the stage for the "underground Church"—Catholics who formed cells and groups for worship and social action, declaring themselves outside the authority and constraints of the institutional Church.

The high point of 1967 was the act of Daniel and Philip Berrigan—one a Jesuit priest, the other a Josephite priest—in pouring blood on the files of the Selective Service in Baltimore.[22] The counterpoint to this deed took place across the continent in Los Angeles, where Cardinal McIntyre began his struggle with the Sisters of the Immaculate Heart of Mary over the extent and forms of their order's postconciliar renewal.[23] The ensuing months unfolded one of the classic sagas of postconciliar confrontation in U.S. Catholicism. In the end, this religious order of women was dismantled.

Another confrontation, but one of many similar occurrences during this period, was the accusation by Archbishop Lucy of San Antonio, Texas, that the Jesuit biblical scholar Father John L. McKenzie was a heretic.

A story by Colman McCarthy in the *National Catholic Reporter* in December 1967 discussed the Trappists. This contemplative order of men was not spared the decline in vocations nor the departure of monks from their ranks that other religious orders had been experiencing. McCarthy pointed out that the number of Trappists had declined from one thousand in 1955 to six hundred in 1965. The reasons for this crisis, said McCarthy, could be traced to an "outmoded and un-Christian life."[24]

Racial issues, poverty, and, of course, the war dominated the news during the following year, 1968. Catholics that year read about some Maryknoll missionaries in Guatemala who became guerrillas against the government. Missionary work itself was being questioned. Was not this importation of Catholicism by U.S. missionaries into foreign countries just another imperialistic advance? With the burning social issues—and the burning inner cities—that characterized 1968, one is not surprised to read an article in the *National Catholic Reporter* (by the Rev. John F. Mahoney) entitled, "Is Convent Life Fundamentally Un-Christian?"[25] This was the year of the Poor People's March on Washington, D.C. At a reunion of the alumni of the North American College, that Roman training ground for most of the future U.S. bishops, some priests interrupted the normally placid, convivial proceedings in order to introduce a resolution in support of Father James Groppi and one in favor of making financial contributions to the poor.[26]

These events, this increasing strife in U.S. Catholicism, caused Protestant theologian Martin Marty to comment that the thrust of renewal in the U.S. Catholic Church was extreme in embracing the secular world and in romanticizing it. Renewal theology, he claimed, was fickle and nervous: it offered experiment as solution, tentative steps as the "last word." Much of this, said Marty, was the working out, in the arena of the U.S. Catholic Church, of the personal problems of priests, religious, and other Catholics involved in radical positions.[27]

"I love you. I need you. I long to be with you. We were made for each other. Forever." An excerpt from a letter of a husband or wife to an absent spouse? No . . . an excerpt from a letter of a seminarian to his girlfriend. In July 1968, an article on seminarians dating—a phenomenon called by various names: "a companionship," "a dialogue," "a now-centered relationship," "an encounter in Christ," "a mutual renewal," "relating," "the third way"—told of the large numbers in training in religious orders and seminaries who were having intense, personal relationships with those of the opposite sex.[28] It is no wonder that the *Official Catholic Directory* for that year reported the first decline of the number of priests in the United States since 1940.

But it was the issuance of July 29, 1968, of the encyclical *Humanae Vitae* by Pope Paul VI, forbidding artificial birth control, that sparked the major controversy of postconciliar Catholicism.[29] Very few of the U.S. bishops attempted to justify the encyclical; but at the same time, they did not speak out against it. Numerous theologians, priests, religious, and laity, in baffled surprise that the pope would have gone against the overwhelming opinion of the papal commission on this matter, excoriated the pope and the curial officials who allegedly prompted his action. Polls and surveys indicated that the vast majority of U.S. priests and Catholic laity rejected the pope's teaching, and that a substantial majority of Catholic married couples were using contraception in their marital relations. Indeed, the dilemma of an official Church teaching that was ignored by the bulk of those to whom it was directed remains a problem for the Church today.

This action of Pope Paul VI—visible as it was—focused the issue of papal and hierarchical authority in the Church. It also produced a further problem of credibility; but to say that it was the cause of U.S. Catholic disintegration is to overlook the unfolding events of the previous four years.

The pages of the *National Catholic Reporter* in 1968 continued to chronicle the strife and the disintegration in U.S. Catholicism. There was a report that 430 Catholic grammar and high schools were closed between 1966 and 1968. There were news stories on the departure from the priesthood of the Jesuit provincial of the order's Maryland province, Father William Sponga, to marry a divorcee with three children,[30] and of "the drawing nun" Sister Corita Kent, leaving after thirty-two years as a nun.[31] Fifty-one priests asked for the resignation of Archbishop Robert Lucey.[32] He in turn fired four seminary professors.[33] Cardinal O'Boyle of Washington, D.C., suspended forty-one priests for their views in favor of birth control.[34] One hundred priests staged a demonstration and sit-in at the semi-annual conference of U.S. bishops.[35] And black Catholics called for all-black seminaries.[36] James Forman demanded $500 million from the U.S. Catholic Church in reparation for the wrongs done to blacks.[37]

Catholic churches were not spared the demonstrations that became so much a part of U.S. society at this time. There were Catholic pickets in front of New York's St. Patrick's Cathedral, and police were called in to remove antiwar priests and laity seeking to conduct an "antiwar mass" in Cleveland's St. John's Cathedral.

Radical Catholic theologian Rosemary Ruether called for the "start of some kind of parallel structure [to the institutional Church] that can begin to reform truly."[39]

There were also more departures from the priesthood, among them that of Monsignor Ivan Illich, whose writings and Center for Inter-Cultural Documentation in Cuernavaca, Mexico, had made him well-known in the United States,[39] and Bishop James Shannon, who was a favorite with liberal Catholics.[40]

Liturgical conferences became less concerned with discussions on liturgical renewal than with issuing radical pronouncements and entertaining their conferees with rock bands. The *National Catholic Reporter* captured the mood of the 1969 national conference with an article entitled "Liturgy Week Blows Mind."[41]

An article by James Degnan in *Christianity Today* was discussed in a December 1969 issue of the *National Catholic Reporter*. Commenting on an article entitled "What Is a Catholic?" in the January 1968 issue of *Look*, Degnan opposed those contributors to the article who took away any distinctive meaning in being a Catholic. Such phrases as "Being a Catholic is the experience of human unity related in one way or another toward the person of Jesus of Nazareth," and, "Belonging to the Catholic Church is not determined by sociological or sacramental criteria but by one's awareness of community" were, Degnan contended, meaningless.[42]

The last shreds of civility in the continuing strife in U.S. Catholicism seemed to disappear in 1969. The Chicago Conference of Laymen censured its executive director, Donald Nicodemus, for using obscenities in a discussion with the auxiliary bishop of Chicago, John May, during a meeting.[43]

Catholic schools continued under pressure. A report indicated that there had been a 25 percent decline in the number of priests, nuns, and brothers teaching in Catholic schools from 1965-1966 to 1969. Some 1,355 Catholic schools had been closed between 1965 and 1970—531 of these being closed between the school years of 1968-1969 and 1969-1970.[44]

The raw figures on U.S. Catholicism showed continued decline in the beginning of the 1970s; there were forty thousand seminarians in 1966, only 23,800 in 1970;[45] a Gallup poll reported that 71 percent of Catholics went to mass on Sundays in 1964, while only 57 percent did so in 1971.[46] And the *Official Catholic Directory* reported that 1970 was the first time in the twentieth century that the population of U.S. Catholics had declined. The National Opinion Research Council (NORC) reported that 3,413 diocesan and religious priests left the priesthood between 1966 and 1969 (half in the latter year).[47] Between 1965 and 1972, according to another report, some twenty thousand nuns had left their religious orders. Sociologists William McCready and Andrew Greeley released a study indicating that attendance at weekly mass had declined to 48 percent of Catholics, that the percentage of those who never attended had increased to 14 percent, and that there were signs that attendance at mass by middle-aged and older Catholics was also declining.[49] The same study showed that Catholic approval of abortion was increasing and that there was substantial erosion of confidence in the leadership of the U.S. Catholic Church.[50] By 1973-1974, there were only 17,334 seminarians.[51]

The same theological battles and ecclesiastical donnybrooks that marked the second half of the 1960s carried over into the 1970s. Louis Evely, a former French priest whose books were popular in the United States, wrote a book in which he claimed that the Lord's Prayer, the "Our Father," teaches error.[52]

Nine nuns who taught at St. Raymond's Parish School, in St. Louis, Missouri, got up at a Sunday mass and told the startled congregation that they were quitting as teachers in the school because the members of the parish were un-Christian and racist.[53] Dr. Harry J. McSorley, a laicized, married former priest and recognized expert on Martin Luther, was removed by Catholic bishops from his position on a commission involved in Catholic-Lutheran ecumenical discussions.[54] A photo in the *National Catholic Reporter* showed two policemen dragging away, under arrest, Father John Egan of Newark, New Jersey, for demonstrating at a meeting of U.S. bishops.[55] Cardinal Humberto Medeiros of Boston fired a Jesuit campus minister at Harvard University, and in reply to student protests responded, "The laity now do not have a say in the appointment of priests, and I think it will be a sad day when they do."[56]

By the mid-1970s, the turmoil lessened. Bishop-baiting stopped. The number of seminarians and those in religious orders stabilized. Fewer priests and religious were leaving their vocations. There was a leveling off in mass attendance and devotional practices among Catholics. The fiery radical theologians were mute: their violent dissent from traditional Catholic theological beliefs was no longer trumpeted by the media, and they seemed to float off into other preoccupations. The quality of bishops in the United States improved somewhat with the appointment of Archbishop Jadot as apostolic delegate to the United States.

But the toll on U.S. Catholicism of the volcanic tumult of the decade from the mid-1960s to the mid-1970s—in terms of the traditional historical U.S. Catholic Church—was catastrophic. In 1965 there were 14,296 Catholic schools in the United States with an enrollment of 3,505,186; by 1975 the number of schools had decreased by 25 percent and enrollment had fallen by 35 percent to 2,959,788.[57] In 1965, 14 percent of the grammar school children in the country were in Catholic schools; by 1975 this number had fallen to 8 percent.[58]

The sociologists who compiled the survey that is the basis for *Catholic Schools in a Declining Church* (1976) made this statement in regard to Catholic religious devotion:

> There has been a decline in most measures of religious devotion. Seventy-one percent reported weekly mass attendance in *The Education of Catholic Americans* ( . . . 1966); that proportion has now fallen to 50 percent. Monthly confession has declined from 38 to 17 percent. (Those going to church "practically never" or "not at all" have increased from 18 to 30 percent.) Visits to the church to pray at least once a week have declined from 23 to 15 percent, and daily private prayer has fallen from 72 to 60 percent. The proprotion who "never pray," however, remains low at 4 percent, and the proportion who pray at least once a week continues to be a quite high 82 percent.
>
> Many of the traditional forms of religious behavior have also declined. The percentage of Catholics attending a retreat within the last two years has fallen from 7 percent to 4 percent; making a Day of Recollection, from 22 percent to 9 percent; making a mission, from 34 percent to 6 percent; reading a Catholic maga-

zine or newspaper, from 61 to 56 percent; and having a religious conversation with a priest, from 24 to 20 percent.[59]

The same survey reported substantial shifts in doctrinal belief. In 1963, the authors found, 70 percent thought it was "certainly true" that Jesus handed over the leadership of His church to Peter and the popes; ten years later that proportion had fallen to 42 percent; and by 1973, only 32 percent thought it was "certainly true" that the pope is infallible when he speaks on matters of faith and morals.[60]

The authors of *Catholic Schools in a Declining Church* also polled on matters of personal faith:

> . . . Only 38 percent say that they feel "very sure" when they speak to their children about religious beliefs and values. In 1973, 27 percent of the Catholics thought that it was "certainly true" that God would punish the evil for all eternity, a decline of 25 percentage points in the last decade. Thirty-eight percent thought it was "certainly true" that the Devil existed, while 26 percent thought it was "probably true."[61]

The statistics quoted above do not tell the whole story. For more than a decade the U.S. Catholic Church was buffeted by the winds of change. The responses to the resulting ferment in the Church varied. Some laypersons, like John Cogley, a former editor of *Commonweal*, formally joined other churches. Others drifted away from traditional Catholic practices: in another time they would have been called "lapsed" Catholics. Still others, from habit, duty, or commitment, continued to attend mass weekly, say the rosary, and participate in other Catholic devotional practices. Finally, a small percentage plunged into active involvement in a changed, and changing, Catholic Church. Wherever one was in this spectrum, however, there seemed to be no doubt that the U.S. Church had lost its vitality, had lost a great deal of the loyalty of its members, and had failed in the task mandated by the Second Vatican Council: the spiritual renewal of the Church.

The dormant, apathetic qualities of the postconciliar U.S. Catholic Church are illustrated by the collapse of U.S. Catholic publishing during the late 1960s and early 1970s. *Ave Maria, Jubilee, Critic, Extension,* and numerous other Catholic publications died. Sheed and Ward and Herder and Herder—two prominent Catholic publishing firms—had to be sold because of financial anemia. The Chicago housewife who read *Extension* and the Boston lawyer who read *Jubilee* just didn't seem to care anymore. The readers of such Catholic writers as Chesterton, Belloc, and Maritain, who had been published by Frank Sheed and Maisie Ward, seemed to evaporate.

The penchant for the latest fad and fashion—a characteristic of the era of which we are speaking in almost every aspect of U.S. society—bred an infinite number of experiments in U.S. Catholicism. The Baltimore Catechism was considered outmoded, and so it was supplanted by catechetic instruction materials that took into account contemporary pedagogical advances. The traditional Tridentine mass was now thought to be archaic, and so mimes and rock bands were introduced as part of the liturgy. An example of radical change in Catholic schools is the evolution of the now-defunct San Francisco College for Women (popularly known as Lone Mountain College). A college for girls of upper-middle-class Catholic families, taught by the Religious of the Sacred Heart (popularly called the Madames of the Sacred Heart), this institution was known for its proper, white-gloved students and a strong commitment to a Christian liberal arts education. By the mid-1960s, however, the nuns who ran the college felt that its educational and behavioral standards had become outmoded. They allowed the school to become what one alumna called a "hippie coven." In 1978, as most other institutions of higher learning were attempting to return to higher educational standards and as more and more students were seeking the kind of Catholic and humanist education on which the San Francisco College for Women had once prided itself, it was forced to close its doors.

The controversies that split the U.S. Catholic Church so badly during the 1960s and 1970s were marked by juvenile and intransigent behavior on the part of all parties. The hierarchy, on the whole, displayed bad judgment and inept leadership. They seemed confused and lost; and they responded to the increasing tumult either by closing their eyes to it and allowing any form of experimentation to exist, or by becoming grand inquisitors. The Catholic University imbroglio over the rector's firing of Father Charles Curran, the expulsion of seminarians for picketing Cardinal Cushing, the firing of seminary professors by Archbishop Lucey, the hypocrisy of the hierarchy as a whole in response to *Humanae Vitae,* and the hierarchy's inability to guide the Church are but a few examples of the episcopal blundering which occurred during this troubled period. Some of the hierarchy, reminiscent of the story of the pope, who when asked what he was going to do during his papacy responded, "I am going to enjoy it," seemed to do exactly that. Cardinal William Baum only gave up the idea of residing in a $525,000 house in Washington's posh Embassy Row section after outraged public opinion shamed him out of doing so.

But if the hierarchy were the "heavies," many Catholic priests, nuns, brothers, and laypersons became the "crazies." Whether it was a matter of ecclesiastical or religious concern—liturgical renewal, authority in the Church, the use of contraception—or the role of Catholics in social and racial concerns, a minority of Catholics in the United States, often encouraged by extensive media exposure, felt the call to revolutionary excesses. Whether it was Rosemary Ruether's call for a parallel structure to Catholicism that could truly be a reforming institution, Philip Berrigan's waffling on support of violence among revolutionaries in Latin America while advocating nonviolence in the United States, a group of Jesuits calling for a commitment to Marxism and Maoism, the denial of traditional doctrines of Catholicism, demonstrations in churches, or the excoriation of the bulk of U.S. Catholics for being "unenlightened" and "un-Christian" because they didn't share the same outlook on various political matters, the results of this determination on the part of the few to impose the latest, most fashionable, most shocking concepts or deeds on the majority of U.S. Catholics must be counted one of the most sudden revolutions in history. It was as if priests and religious had suddenly discovered that for years they had been too docile, too pious, too much under the control of superiors and now had to throw off all shackles of restraint. "Narrow" religious concerns—teaching in parish schools, staffing hospitals, serving parishes—seemed too limited in scope. "To the barricades" became the cry; and what began as a sincere concern for social, racial, and even ecclesiastical problems became, because of the demands of an ever-thirsty press, an increasingly radical protest fueled by the glare of publicity. Reform became an umbrella for every sensational fad that came along. Martin Marty's warning that "whenever it issues in fanaticisms, obsession, or crusading spirit, renewal appears not as renewal of Church but as representation of personal problems" became all too real.[63]

The excesses of the radicals of U.S. Catholicism of the past decade and a half have been extensively chronicled—most notably by Dr. James Hitchcock and Father Andrew Greeley. As a new brand of authoritarianism replaced the closed, rigid preconciliar rule by Rome and by the hierarchy, secular politics replaced the concern and action for the social betterment of mankind that *arises from* a spiritual deepening. Profound theological questions were debated in violent, polemical arguments in the popular press. Those who disagreed with the radical pronouncements of theologians were "excommunicated," read out of the Church as "un-Christian." Priests and religious who left their vocations were characterized as the "best and the brightest."

What of the response of the mass of U.S. Catholics to the ferment in the Church that followed the Second Vatican Council? There was much sympathy and support for the reforms inaugurated by the council. Certainly, as it progressed, U.S. Catholics felt that their spiritual lives would be augmented by the new spirit the council presaged. Gradually, however, this promised reform and renewal came to seem aborted to most Catholics. Already stunned by the drastic social changes that occurred in the late 1960s and early 1970s, the changes in Catholicism produced further disequilibrium.

In reading fifteen years of the *National Catholic Reporter* at one fell swoop, I was struck by what many Catholics must have felt from the mid-1960s to the mid-1970s. The priests and nuns, whom they had revered, cherished, and set apart from other men and women since childhood, were suddenly wearing ordinary clothing, criticizing bishops and even the pope, participating in demonstrations, getting arrested, and leaving the Church and getting married. No longer did theologians debate the Virgin Birth, papal infallibility, or the nature of authority in the Church in obscure theological journals or in technical tomes; now *Time* and *Newsweek*, just to name two popular magazines, aired Hans Küng's rather revolutionary thoughts on papal infallibility. The mass and devotions that Catholics had always known had somehow disappeared. Catholic schools were closing by the hundreds.

German Catholics in Milwaukee, Polish Catholics in Chicago, and Irish Catholics in Boston had been raised to be super-patriots in order to show that they could be both loyal Catholics and loyal U.S. citizens. Now priests and nuns were saying that the U.S. involvement in Vietnam was immoral, and were breaking the law and getting arrested to make their point. What is more, in doing so they were thereby supporting a communist regime; and Catholics had been in the forefront of U.S. cold-war opposition to communism.

Many Catholics had just emerged from the ghetto and moved to more affluent neighborhoods, were sending their children to Catholic schools and colleges, and were beginning to enjoy the benefits of the American Dream for which they and their parents had strived so long. And now priests and nuns were telling them that these achievements were un-Christian, that they were racist, that their children should be bused out of their neighborhoods to school, that the local Catholic schools should be closed, that they were guilty not only for the plight of the blacks in the United States but for the lot of the poor in the United States and throughout the world.

Given the strong clerical basis of U.S. Catholicism and the unchanging quality of the Catholic Church prior to the Second Vatican Council, the events that transpired in the Church in the United States in the decade following the council caused confusion, anger, and dismay to the bulk of U.S. Catholics. These events were also a major factor in causing the precipitous decline in mass attendance, devotional practices, and what can be called orthodox thinking among Catholics.

While the Second Vatican Council may have taken place just prior to one of the most convulsive decades in U.S. history by coincidence, and while much of what has come to be called conciliar thinking or "the spirit of Vatican II" had no basis in the conciliar documents, the upheavals in U.S. Catholicism would probably have occurred even if the council had not been held. The children and grandchildren of immigrant Catholics were now part of the mainstream of U.S. life: they partook in the countercultural swirls of the times. Religion—with the exception of such exotic manifestations as the occult, tarot, and I Ching, and various Eastern religious practices—played little or no role in their lives. The movements of heightened consciousness—women's liberation, the explosive concern about human sexuality, the human potential movement—caused Catholics and non-Catholics alike to question the values with which they had been brought up. At about the same time, the spiraling divorce rate in the United States caught up with Catholics, who had been conservative relative to the rest of the country in the matter of divorce. While it cannot be stated unequivocally that divorce and remarriage has caused Catholics to lapse from the active practice of Catholicism, it has probably been a major reason for the decline in mass attendance and devotional practice. The analogy between the end of a marriage that was supposed to be "forever" and the loss of the unchanging characteristics of Catholicism has probably been instrumental in causing more than a few Catholics to lapse from active religious practices. Further, the proclivity for more and more Catholics not to marry other Catholics—particularly after a divorce—has also lessened Catholic practice.

By the mid-1970s, when the United States began a "return to normalcy," when the pendulum began to swing away from the radical eruptions of the second half of the 1960s and the early 1970s, when religion (as most visibly experienced by the fundamentalist Protestant churches) began to be a major factor in U.S. society, the U.S. Catholic Church was severely troubled. Its leadership remained stunned from the vicissitudes of the previous decade. Priests and religious who remained after the ravaged vocations of that decade either felt powerless or had been trained in the laissez-faire times of the previous several years. No one seemed able to reconstruct the U.S. Catholic Church.

Liberal and radical Catholics claimed that the "best" seminarians, priests, nuns, and brothers had left their vocations. This assertion is impossible to prove or disprove. It is true that many bright, talented, concerned, and committed priests and religious did leave their vocations. Reasons for these departures were varied: failure to find fulfillment in the priestly or religious life, a desire to marry, a feeling that the secular life would be more meaningful and would afford a larger arena of endeavor, a belief that the Church was not reforming rapidly enough. The reasons given, however, were often not the ones that had truly motivated those who were departing; and many Catholics became quite sceptical of the high-minded explanations that many priests and religious gave for leaving their vocations when they learned that these same priests and religious had married soon after departing.

There seems to be no comprehensive data on the lives of these priests and religious after they left their vocations. Most disappeared from view, finding jobs in business, government bureaucracies, and in academia; marrying, divorcing—in short, becoming indistinguishable from most other citizens of the United States. Some, like William Du Bay, whose rebellion against Cardinal McIntyre of Los Angeles was one of the first incidents in U.S. Catholicism that signaled the coming tumult, occasionally surfaced in the news: first, when he married; second, when he declared that he was a homosexual.

The dreams of many former priests and religious to carry on their selected ministries as laypersons have rarely come to fruition. One priest, who claimed that he was leaving the priesthood in order to devote more of his time to the poor, married a former nun, had two children, divorced, and is now a life insurance salesman.

Surprisingly, there were few rumblings among the Catholic laity regarding their payments for the new lifestyle of priests and religious during the past decade-and-a-half. When the Jesuit community at the University of San Francisco bought a four-unit apartment house for $600,000 to accommodate three or four Jesuits who wished to live in a smaller community, lay contributors to the Society of Jesus didn't seem to grumble. When priests and religious with expensive educations, paid for by the Catholic faithful, left their vocations, the issue was never discussed. Nor was the matter of the increased sums now necessary to train, maintain, and educate priests and religious.

When fashionably dressed nuns travel to Florida to speak to a convention in favor of abortion, however, one begins to wonder not only about the religious principles involved, but also about the economics of the "renewal" of religious life.

There have been numerous theories for the susceptibility of the U.S. Catholic Church to the virulent faddism of the 1960s and 1970s. Some authors have castigated the writings of the Jesuit scientist and theologian, Teilhard de Chardin, for the secular bent of Catholicism during the postconciliar period. One of these authors, John Eppstein, in a work highly critical of the Church in the postconciliar decade, *Has the Catholic Church Gone Mad?*, states:

> It seems evident that . . . Father Teilhard de Chardin . . . is the father of the New Theology. Every one of the major tendencies which we observe today, except the common toadying to the prevailing obsession and to democracy [within the Church] . . . is to be found in his writings. . . . There is the almost idolatrous belief in progress. This is the notion that evolution is the secret of the universe and that traditional Christian doctrine must be trimmed or developed to fit it. There is in consequence the emphasis on "becoming" rather than "being." This, and the notion of sin as simply one of the elements which inevitably make up the complex universe as a statistical necessity, operate against the direct moral relationship of each man, woman and child with God. There is the mission to achieve a new world religion free from the fetters of the old. There is the superior contempt of the *illuminati*, who imagine that they have this mission, for the reaching and ruling functions of the Church's magisterium, Papal pronouncements included.[65]

Even if, as Eppstein and Garry Wills state, Teilhard de Chardin unwittingly fathered the New Theology—with its worship of the secular and its greater freedom in questioning papal author-

ity in matters of faith and morals—there is little reason to believe that his influence was felt in the Catholic rank and file,
whether among the laity, priests, or religious. It is true that during the 1960s Teilhard de Chardin was almost a culture hero, his
name on everyone's lips—Catholic and non-Catholic alike.
There were seminars and workshops to examine his thought.
His books were bestsellers. But one can justifiably assert that
very few understood his thought sufficiently to draw out its implications for the New Theology. It is unlikely that Teilhard de
Chardin can be considered the "evil genius" behind the tumult
in U.S. Catholicism in the postconciliar decade. As society has
come increasingly to see the limitations of the secular world, the
totalitarian implications of an ever-growing technology, Teilhard de Chardin has been accordingly criticized; and his writings have been lambasted for supporting too much reliance on
the benefactions of "the world." The thought of Teilhard de
Chardin was seized and popularized because society in the 1960s
saw the size and efficiency of the secular arm, the state, as providing all answers to human needs.

The saga of U.S. Catholicism from the closing days of the Second Vatican Council to the mid-1970s is a chronicle of divisive-
ness and change. Restive priests and religious, once genial Father O'Malleys and kindly Sister Bernadettes, became
firebrands, challenging every aspect of society, confronting both
secular and ecclesiastical authority. A minority of the laity
joined them. The majority either drifted away from the traditional practices and beliefs that marked a Catholic, or, docilely
but unenthusiastically, adhered to their religious practices despite the bewildering changes.

Intransigent, unimaginative bishops, more concerned with le-
galisms than with the pastoral care of their flocks, compounded
the problems that arose during this period; and theologians
seemed more intent on garnering headlines than in elucidating
Catholic doctrine.

It was a period of unprecedented chaos for U.S. Catholicism—
a period which future historians will probably consider as sig-

nificant for the U.S. Catholic Church as the eighteenth century, during which the Enlightenment ravaged Catholic Europe, or the nineteenth century, when the Church lost the industrial workers of Europe.

# 6/ The Liturgical Crisis

... *We must speak plainly: there is practically no liturgy worthy of the name today in the Catholic Church. Yesterday's liturgy was hardly more than an embalmed cadaver. What people call liturgy today is little more than this same cadaver decomposed.* LOUIS C. BOUYER, The Decomposition of Catholicism

It is the late 1960s. About forty persons have gathered for mass on a Sunday afternoon in the dining room of a large house that serves as one of the dormitories for a Catholic college. Homemade posters and banners hang on the walls; the dining room table has been converted into an altar; the priest wears a sports shirt, and some of the nuns present wear bermuda shorts; the Epistle is a passage from the *New York Times* (Sunday edition, of course); the Gospel is taken from the writings of Daniel Berrigan, with bongo drums beating in the background; a Beatles song serves as an Introit, and a partially clad woman student, who is an accomplished jazz dancer, cavorts about at the Offertory. The homily is a collective effort: at its beginning, several marijuana cigarettes are lighted and passed around, and almost all of those present will offer a few thoughts before or after taking a "hit."

In a Los Angeles suburb, a young priest organizes "home masses" in the early evenings. It is the cocktail hour, he reasons, that is today's liturgical expression—rather than going to a church for mass. Nor do bread and wine have the same meaning to people today as they did two thousand years ago. Therefore, at these "home masses," he has substituted whiskey and Ry-Krisp for the no-longer-meaningful bread and wine.

At a church on New York's Upper West Side, the pews have been removed and replaced by huge pillows. A priest attired as a clown walks into the church accompanied by several guitar-strumming and bongo-beating young men and women festooned with flowers and strands of crepe paper. Mass proceeds with readings from the writings of Mao Tse-tung and Che Guevara. A light show begins during the Offertory, reaches a dazzling peak during the Consecration, and diminishes in intensity after Communion. At the conclusion of mass, worshipers form a ring by holding hands. Dancing around the coffee table that has served as an altar, they move faster and faster to the rock music being played by the handful of musicians in the center of the circle. Finally the music ends. Some spin off in dizzy individuality; some form small groups clutching each other in tight embrace; a few sob, others laugh uproariously.

In a newly built church in an upper-middle-class parish in San Mateo, California, the pastor presides over the mass while perched on a gilt chair situated on a dais. A neon sign behind him flashes instructions—"SIT," "STAND," "KNEEL"—to the congregation. A saccharine hymn sung by a choir of crack-voiced matrons provides musical background for the Kiss of Peace—a ritual accomplished by those in the congregation turning to others sitting near them, flashing manifestly insincere smiles, and mouthing the word "peace."

These are but a few examples of the liturgical experimentation—and liturgical realities—that have occurred since the Second Vatican Council promulgated the "Constitution on the Sacred Liturgy" in December 1963. Experimentation largely came to an end in 1970, with the implementation of Pope Paul VI's new *Ordo Missae.* For many, what followed was a liturgical wasteland, and Pope Paul's attempt to impose some liturgical uniformity was blasted as mandating a boring liturgy, more akin to a Presbyterian or Unitarian service than to the glorious Catholic liturgical heritage.

Progressives[1] were dismayed and angered by the pope's predictable call for an end to liturgical experimentation. Conservatives were angered by the discontinuity with liturgical tradition and by what they considered to be an empty and uninspiring liturgy. Probably no aspect of postconciliar Catholicism in the United States has stirred so much controversy as that of liturgical change. Some have even suggested that the substantial decline in attendance at Sunday mass since the mid-1960s is a direct outgrowth of the change in liturgy.

A brief overview of the role of the liturgy in U.S. Catholicism before the Second Vatican Council will be helpful in understanding the chaos that this change has caused in the postconciliar period. "The primary access route to God for a Catholic was the liturgy of the Mass, in which the Sacrament of the Holy Eucharist is celebrated and made available to the Faithful," writes liturgist and theologian George Devine.[2] Devine points out that in antiquity this celebration tended to be intimate, joyous, even somewhat spontaneous; but that as the political unity of the West became increasingly important to the Church, a uniform liturgy began to be imposed by both Church and State throughout Western Europe. As early as A.D. 754, Pepin, father of Charlemagne, decreed that Latin rites other than the main one emanating from Rome would have to be suppressed in his realm. The early Middle Ages witnessed the rise of vernacular languages in Western Europe, and it followed that the Church in the West could not have both a uniform liturgy and a vernacular liturgy. Thus Latin became the liturgical language of uniformity. Many liturgists claim that the Roman liturgy would have been reformed in the sixteenth century had it not been for the polarized atmosphere surrounding the Protestant Reformation. At the Council of Trent, held in the sixteenth century, external signs of stability such as the Latin language were seen as important to preserving the identity of those who remained loyal to the Roman Catholic Church. "Thus for four centuries more," writes Devine, "the liturgy in the Western Church would remain in Latin and would continue to suggest a mysterious division between the sacred mysteries of the altar and the lay congregants in the nave of the church."[3]

Despite such difficulties, as the great Jesuit liturgist Josef A.

Jungmann has remarked, the mass remained the chief source of grace for the Church. Although many of the lines of communication between layman and altar were indirect and required a number of supports, the piety of the Church continued to revolve around the celebration of the Eucharist.

The hordes of simple, unlettered Catholic immigrants who came to the United States during the nineteenth and twentieth centuries had known this traditional mass in the villages of Europe. Whatever their attitudes to the mass had been, once the immigrants settled in the urban ghettos of the United States the mass became for them both a symbol of ethnic religious continuity and a practicality of community during the brief Sunday surcease from work and household tasks.

The fact that the Catholic immigrant in the United States was generally satisfied to attend mass whenever obliged to do so (on Sundays and prescribed holy days of obligation), and in many cases more often, meant that he or she was not concerned about the intelligibility of the ritual. What mattered was sacramental efficacy. Although more educated laypersons might own and use a missal (a small, hand-held edition in English of the *Missale Romanum* that the priest used at the altar), most Catholics opted for less direct means of "praying the mass." Devine points out:

> For some it was the Rosary, for others a prayerbook (distinct from the missal in that it was a generic prayerbook, not just a book of liturgical texts), for others a series of favorite personal prayers known by heart, and for still others a practice as old as the venerable churches of Europe: meditation on the mysteries of the faith . . . aided by church architecture, statuary, stained glass, and other liturgical arts. . . . More often than not, the Mass became a vehicle for such indirect routes to God as the veneration of the Virgin or of a particular Saint . . . often signified by praying before a statue . . . or even by lighting of a vigil light before the statue. . . .[4]

Liturgical renewal began to be called for in the early years of the twentieth century. Pope Pius X asked for a renewal of liturgical piety, including frequent reception of Communion and greater intelligibility in the liturgy. Popes Pius XI and Pius XII stressed the same themes; and the dialogue mass came into being in some parishes. The congregation would recite the Latin responses as a group in alternation with the prayers of the priest.

Throughout the 1950s and early 1960s a small group of U.S. Catholics sought liturgical renewal. Many of these efforts centered around making the existing Latin mass a more aesthetically creative experience and thereby a more prayerful experience. Some of those who labored for liturgical renewal sought to have a vernacular mass—or at least to have most of the mass in the vernacular. The promulgation of the "Constitution on the Sacred Liturgy" by the Second Vatican Council was a virtually unexpected canonization of the efforts of these reformers. But what transpired in this liturgical renewal during the remaining years of the 1960s was beyond the wildest imaginings of even the most innovative proponents of liturgical renewal.

During the first few years after the council's decree authorizing changes in the liturgy, liturgical renewal meant leap-frogging to the vernacular "folk" mass. "Once removed from language," writes George Devine, "the American Church removed itself from Rome in ritual atmosphere as well, and the austere, the splendid, the solemn, the carefully executed all seemed to give way to the 'pop,' the streamlined, the 'instant,' the 'funky.' " [5]

Organs gave way to guitars as Latin gave way to English. The stately Gregorian chant was heard no more, replaced by folk hymns like "Take Our Bread (We Love You)," "My Lord will Come Again (. . ."He'll take my hand and we'll go home. . . . "), "We Are Your Bread Now" (to the tune of "Waltzing Matilda"), and "We Are All Joined in Christ" (to the tune of "Edelweiss"). Preconciliar proponents of liturgical reform, especially those enamored of Gregorian chant, were aghast at such banality in liturgical music. As in any revolutionary experience, the initial moderate leaders were swept aside.

There was an almost indecent haste to dismantle every aspect of the traditional rite which had been central to Catholics for at least four hundred years. Tables were set up in the sanctuary, replacing the altar against the wall. The priest now said mass facing the people instead of with his back to them. Bells were no longer rung at the *Sanctus*, the *Hanc igitur*, the Elevation, or the

*Domine, non sum dignus.* More extensive Biblical readings were introduced, and these were often read by laypersons—even women. Communion could be received in the hand; and both the wine and bread were often offered to communicants. Liturgical vestments were simplified—sometimes to the point of disappearance. The symbolism of the ancient liturgy was reduced.

Andrew Greeley characterizes the tendency of the Church in the mid-1960s to strip the rich symbolism of the liturgy:

> At the very time the psychedelics are evolving a new, rich, elaborate, and playful liturgy, we are doing our best to reform ours so that it looks exactly like that kind of Protestant liturgy that was deemed most appropriate for bourgeois industrialism. ... The hippies are putting on vestments, just as we're taking them off. The psychedelics are seeking ecstasy, and we are having group-discussion homilies.[6]

In the decade-and-a-half following the liturgical changes prompted by the Second Vatican Council, attendance at mass by U.S. Catholics began to decline. It would be unfair—and probably untrue—to say that the "new mass" caused this dropping off in obligatory attendance at mass. The causes, as we have seen, were much more complex. Nevertheless, the extraordinarily high percentage of U.S. Catholics who had attended Sunday mass regularly (possibly the highest percentage of any country in the world) before the mid-1960s slowly began to erode.

What went wrong? Why were the high hopes of those who had for so long pushed for a more meaningful liturgy, a more theologically sensitive liturgy, dashed? Rather than stimulating a renewal of liturgical piety, the "new Mass" seemed to alienate an increasing number of U.S. Catholics. One reason for this negative response to the liturgical changes following the Second Vatican Council was the lack of preparation. The changes in the liturgy were not supposed to have been a jolt for anyone: they were supposed to have been a smooth transition into a new liturgical piety in the Church which would have been truer to authentic Catholic tradition. However, although the Decree of the Sacred Liturgy from the Second Vatican Council called for careful preparations of the clergy and the laity in advance of the liturgical renovations, this rarely took place. Instead, there was a minimum of instruction in the mechanics of change, without adequate psychological preparation for the fact that the Church was suddenly going to change something that it had told people for years was *never* going to be changed. And, despite the fact that these changes were incidental to the dogma of the Church, they were not incidental to the psychology of Catholics. For them, the traditional mass was a way of relating symbolically, of acting out in ritual a deep and complex faith-relationship that could not be understood abstractly nearly so well as it could be ritualized concretely.

The implementation of the Second Vatican Council's "Constitution on the Sacred Liturgy" that brought about the liturgical changes during the second half of the 1960s, intended to take the mystification out of the Roman liturgy, but seemed to many to take out the mystery as well. The theological underpinnings of the new liturgy, although quite sound, were used to construct what most Catholics considered a barren ceremony. There was a failure to understand that historical intersecting between the liturgy and drama. Such commentators as Garry Wills and James Hitchcock have maintained that the mistake was in taking away a set of symbolic ways of relating to the mass without installing another set that would be equally serviceable, or in taking care to preserve as many elements from the old set as possible. It is obvious that a wide chasm existed between the liturgical experts, entrusted with formulating the liturgical changes, and the mainstream of U.S. Catholics.

Reactions to the changes varied. Once the novelty of innovation and experimentation had worn off, very few Catholics seemed enthusiastic about the replacement for the traditional Tridentine mass.[7] British author John Eppstein scathingly denounced the changes that had taken place in both the mass and the divine office in his book, *Has The Catholic Church Gone Mad?*[8] And Garry Wills commented:

> So the shock of adjustment was greatest when the Mass was tampered with. Any new thing here posed the whole problem of change in its most poignant form. The layman, coming home,

found it a strange house, cluttered with signs of an alien occupancy. He was asked to do things against which elaborate inhibitions had been built up all his life. . . . [9]

In one of the most perceptive analyses on the new liturgy, James Hitchcock wrote:

The new liturgy, whether by design or accident, seems especially ineffective in conveying to worshippers a sense of transcendence and deep spirituality. Prayers and readings have a straightforward and matter-of-fact quality devoid of deep reverberations or memorable rhythms. [10]

In the United States, most of the older Catholics continued regular Sunday mass observance in a "grin-and-bear-it" manner. They fiddled with the plethora of "missalettes" that had supplanted their leather-bound *Saint Andrew Daily Missal*, and made conscious efforts to get used to the "new mass." Others began to attend mass less frequently. Still others sought a church that offered a more meaningful liturgy. Such churches were usually staffed by younger priests and had as their principal attraction a sense of intimacy and community. Those Catholics who became involved in experimental liturgy during the 1960s—sometimes in the form of "home masses" or the so-called "underground mass"—found during the 1970s that this was a liturgical "dead end." The movement began rapidly to wither. And some conservative Catholics reacted to the liturgical changes by seeking centers where the more familiar rites could be continued. [11]

That the liturgical renewal ushered in by Vatican Council II did not deliver all it promised—or perhaps not even most of what it promised—can be attributed to a number of factors, which can be summarized as follows: (1) too much was expected from vernacularization and from other liturgical changes; (2) the inadequate preparation of the Catholic community for the changes; (3) the conception of liturgical changes in such "hothouse" environments as monasteries; (4) a reluctance or inability to implement liturgical changes on the part of both clergy and laity; (5) the inability of liturgists to implement their own proposals; and (6) the lack of consistency and economy in introducing change.

Before the Second Vatican Council, the U.S. Catholic Church (like the Church throughout the world) had been nurtured on the sentiment that "the Church never changes." That this is theologically correct as far as the Deposit of Faith (the body of truths as taught by Christ) is concerned cannot be denied; but, as Cardinal Newman has so brilliantly pointed out, the understanding or consciousness of the Deposit of Faith develops over a period of time. Although the liturgical changes following the Second Vatican Council were sound and desirable from a theological point of view, the psychological, emotional, and spiritual consequences of these changes jolted and shocked U.S. Catholics. There may have been no theoretical justification for this; but the threat to the accustomed liturgical stability of U.S. Catholics was a reality. George Devine's assessment can be fruitfully quoted:

> ... In matters liturgical ... there must obtain a certain economy of change, a certain judicious appropriation of the psychological and emotional—as well as intellectual and physical—resources people are able to bring to a situation that demands change, so as to effect those changes which are most needed. This will often mean leaving in abeyance those areas of change which are also desirable, but far less crucial for the time being.[12]

Any consideration of the liturgical crisis as an aspect of U.S. Catholicism following the Second Vatican Council must consider the role of the liturgy in the life of this Catholic community. We have seen the central importance of the mass in the lives of Catholics before the council: surveys tell us that today more and more U.S. Catholics are not going to mass and to the sacraments. The experience of watching long lines of Catholics outside of confessionals on Saturdays in churches through the United States is a thing of the past. Although new forms of liturgy and sacramental presentation have contributed to the steady decline in liturgical and sacramental participation by U.S. Catholics, there are other forces at work as well.

One of these, as has been pointed out earlier in this book, is the increasing assimilation of U.S. Catholics into the mainstream of life in this country after World War II. In earlier years, the combination of ethnic and religious separateness had tended to make U.S. Catholics "a people apart." An analogy might be drawn to the Jews in Israel as depicted in the Old Testament: they had their own theocratic state, but were constantly influenced by the polytheistic concepts of groups around them. The distinctive Mosaic Law that governed the Jews was always in danger of being subverted. It was from these dangers that a long succession of prophets called the Jews to worship the One True God. It can be argued that U.S. Catholics, once they became part of the fabric of U.S. life, were no longer as attached to the Church and its liturgy and sacraments as a social force.

Many of those who advocated and structured the liturgical changes of the 1960s were unaware of the psychological and sociological implications of the liturgy in the lives of U.S. Catholics. James Hitchcock observes:

> What the liturgist assumes to have been a boring, meaningless experience was often quite meaningful to many people because they did not so much take meaning from it as bring meaning to it. They believed that something of infinite importance was happening at the altar, and hence to them the experience was not empty. The Latin, and the people's silence, also forced many people to interiorize both their devotions and their understanding of the Eucharist, and if this was perhaps not the ideal form of participation at Mass it was nonetheless a religious exercise which few people now have occasion to go through. . . . Those who think that the old liturgy was irrelevant to life overlook the experience once attainable in large downtown churches, in which persons of the most diverse social classes—impoverished old ladies, policemen on the beat, students, prosperous businessmen, factory laborers—gathered spontaneously for a brief time before returning once more to the world. There was even an unrecognized kind of community here—even if they did not greet each other they shared a common sense of what was happening in the liturgy, and why they were there.[18]

If there is to be any meaningful liturgical renewal in postconciliar U.S. Catholicism, there must be careful consideration of the role of liturgy, of worship, within the framework of community.

This crucible must include extensive evaluation of the symbols and the psychological aspects of the liturgy. George Devine summarizes the need for reexamination:

> What seemed necessary for American Catholics in the area of prayer and liturgy was a serious reexamination of the role of symbols and structures in their worship lives. Any full and honest answers to such questioning had to go significantly beyond the trivial concerns of Latin versus English, organ versus guitar, or the various alternative penitential rites and eucharistic prayers in the *Ordo Missae*. There would have to be reconsideration of the parish community . . . , its role in an age of increasing personal and family mobility, and the role of clergy and laity in its ongoing Christian life.[14]

The psychological aspects of liturgical life should also be considered in any attempts to revive among U.S. Catholics the impetus of liturgical renewal. Although these psychological dimensions pervade every aspect of the liturgy and the sacraments, for me the best example of the failure of the liturgical changes to consider the nature of those who partake in the liturgy is that of the funeral mass. While there is no doubt that the Mass of the Resurrection follows a much more theologically authentic concept, it is my perception that the preconciliar mass for the dead, with its lugubrious sequence, "Dies irae, dies illa," and its hopeful antiphon, "In paradisum," [15] struck a more responsive chord, a more holistic approach, to those who mourned than its replacement. The black vestments, the mournful solemnity of the ritual, the constant symbolism of the passage through death into eternal life—these were calculated to provide an exorcism of grief and of the sense of loss by emphasizing the awesome fact of death. It was a ceremony with a perceptive clarity of humanity's total make-up—which all liturgy should have.

A great deal of work remains to be done in assessing both the historic role of the mass and the sacraments in the lives of U.S. Catholics before the Second Vatican Council and their place in contemporary U.S. Catholicism. It is not within the scope of this book to make specific recommendations about the future of the liturgy nor to explore systematically the current liturgical experience in the United States. (The diversity of the current liturgical experience awaits a commentator.) Nor do I suggest a return to "the good old days" of the Tridentine mass.

The liturgy in postconciliar Catholicism cannot be viewed as separate from the sense of community implied in the Second Vatican Council's exploration of "the People of God." Now that the transitional confusion of the decade following the council seems to be over, now that the shock of the liturgical changes is blunted, and now that the extravagant hopes for liturgical renewal have lapsed into a more realistic experience, it is time for an "agonizing reappraisal" of the role of the liturgy in U.S. Catholicism.

# *second spring:*

## THE COMING OF AGE OF U.S. CATHOLICISM

# 7| Out of the Mainstream: An Examination of the Catholic Charismatic Movement and the Beginnings of Neo-Orthodoxy

It was a clear, star-filled evening. I drove across the bridge from San Francisco to Oakland, and followed the well-written directions that my friend Betty Scully had given me to find Most Holy Redeemer Center, a former seminary for Redemptorist priests, now a Catholic charismatic center.

Catholic charismatics?! Fortunately, I had already experienced this new movement in U.S. Catholicism—once at the University of San Francisco and once at the Benedictine charismatic community in Pecos, New Mexico. I was therefore somewhat prepared for this unusual—for modern Catholicism—manifestation of Christian spirituality.

As I walked into the large hall where the liturgy and prayer meeting were to be held, I was immediately and warmly greeted by a young priest. He questioned me as to how I had happened to come to the service, welcomed me, and invited me to have some coffee. No sooner had he gone on to speak to someone else than a middle-aged couple came up to me, introduced themselves, and welcomed me. And on it went for the next forty-five minutes before the liturgy began.

The joyful effusiveness with which the "regulars" at Most Holy Redeemer Charismatic Center greeted and welcomed me, and the fact that the two hundred persons who had gathered for the liturgy had drawn up their chairs tightly around the make-shift altar made me smile: truly this was a new manifestation in Catholicism. The habits, so noticeable in Catholic churches, of entering and leaving without a word to anyone, of sitting scattered and isolated in every pew in the church, were the antithesis of the sense of community that was at the heart of the eucharistic celebration. Certainly this Catholic gathering was not deficient in this aspect of community: there was a genuine sense of joy and care, for those who attended regularly as well as for those, like myself, who were there for the first time.

A group of guitarists and singers began to play and sing a spirited hymn as three priests and four laypersons came to the altar. Each of those congregated for the liturgy lustily joined in the singing—yet another departure from the usual Catholic experience at mass—reading the hymn from the mimeographed booklet that had been passed out. The readings that began the mass were delivered by the four laypersons; and there was a short period of reflection after each had been read. Each person in the congregation followed the readings in his or her missal, and would occasionally consult the Bible that he or she had brought.

The reflective silence that followed the third reading was broken by a very audible cry, coming from somewhere in back of me. "Oh, Jesus, have mercy on me." "Amen," someone else responded. "Jesus, I love you so much," exclaimed a man sitting in front of me. "Oh, yes. Oh, yes. Oh, yes," someone to my right loudly proclaimed.

It was as if a signal had been given for a babble to erupt from the congregation. At first it was similar to an orchestra tuning up before a performance—cacophonous, yet somehow melodious. It became louder . . . and louder. People in the congregation began standing up with their hands raised on high: their eyes were closed, their faces rapt with ecstasy, unintelligible sounds pouring from their mouths. Suddenly, the sounds began to die down, and there was silence once again. A priest got up to read the Gospel.

The sermon that followed was a remarkable job of explicating all the readings in a single theme and of relating the Scriptural passages to a principal charismatic motif of establishing a personal relationship with Jesus Christ. Simply expressed and articulately rendered, the sermon seemed to be directly aimed, as if in conversation, to each person in the congregation.

There was no collection at the Offertory. Instead, several persons got up and deposited packages of cigarettes, liquor bottles, a pair of crutches, and some bottles of pills in front of the altar. These, I learned later, were signs of the battles to give up vices or symbols of cures that had been gifts from God as a result of the conversion of some of those present. As the offerings were being presented, loud, ecstatic singing was going on; and each person returning to his or her chair was hugged and kissed by those standing nearby.

During the canon of the mass, the entire congregation crowded around the altar; and during the "kiss of peace," rather than the limp handshakes and pallid smiles that usually mark this ritual, there was a bout of joyous hugging, squeezing, and kissing.

After the mass had ended, the evening continued with prayer, scriptural reading, and sharing of experiences. Many of those present read a passage from Scripture, and proceeded to explicate the meaning of the text. Others gave "testimony": told of how they (or someone they knew) had been cured through prayer, of how they had been "converted," or how "baptism in the Spirit" had changed their entire lives.

There was no formal healing that evening; but one woman who had complained of having a migraine headache all day had her head covered with several pairs of hands and was prayed over. A gentleman who was in the throes of a depression was held by three of those present, who kept repeating, "Jesus, Lord," "Jesus, Lord," "Jesus, Lord," while they rocked him back and forth.

An announcement was made that coffee and cookies were being served, and the prayer meeting ended, dissolving into a social gathering. While much of the conversation flowed along mundane, everyday subjects, a good number of those sipping coffee or tea and munching cookies discussed their spiritual exaltation or the problems of family and friends. One young woman, who had been one of the guitarists, sought the prayers of those to whom she was talking for a friend of hers who was a drug addict. A man who appeared to be in his sixties told a couple of listeners how he had happened to be cured of painful arthritis by his prayers. A middle-aged woman proclaimed to the circle around her that her life had been transformed since she became a charismatic: her relationships with her husband, her children, and her friends had improved vastly, her health was better, and she was much happier.

But what seemed most marked—both during the liturgy and prayer meeting and during the socializing at the end of the evening—was the genuine care and concern that those present exhibited toward each other. Those few of us who had never before attended a charismatic gathering at Most Holy Redeemer Center were not excluded from the warmth and concern of the "regulars." Many of the latter group approached me, introduced themselves, and talked with me—all expressing their desire that I return.

It had been a memorable evening—one that was as unusual for me as it would be for most U.S. Catholics.

It all began in February 1967. About twenty persons associated with Duquesne University in Pittsburgh, Pennsylvania, who had been engaged in various liturgical, spiritual, and apostolic endeavors, experienced a profound religious transformation in their lives. This transformation, according to those twenty who had gathered together in prayer when it occurred, meant that they had been brought into real, personal contact with the living Christ. This event was also marked by the appearance of charismatic activity like that known in the early Church: many of those present received the gift of tongues; several received other gifts also, such as prophecy, discernment of spirits, and the power of exorcism.[1]

Within a month what had begun at Duquesne spread to the University of Notre Dame and to the Catholic parish of Michigan State University. From these three centers it spread further: to Cleveland, to the University of Iowa, to the University of Portland in Oregon, and elsewhere. Soon people were speaking of the "Pentecostal movement" in the Catholic Church.

A Pentecostal movement in the Catholic Church? Like the Holy Rollers? Like those storefront Pentecostal churches that drew bemused smiles from Catholics and mainline Protestants alike? Well . . . yes.

What has become one of the most significant and rapidly growing movements in contemporary U.S. Catholicism is also one of the most surprising. Years ago Monsignor Ronald Knox used his considerable literary powers to ridicule such aspects of religion as Pentecostalism in his book, *Enthusiasm*. More recently, two well-known Catholic priests and authors have excoriated the Catholic charismatic movement.[2] Andrew Greeley attacked the movement as early as 1970,[3] and has continued to deplore Catholic Pentecostalism in his many books. The Carmelite leader of the Spiritual Life Institute, William McNamara, writes in *Mystical Passion*:

> Far from being either an appropriate response to or a rejection of divine passion, Pentecostalism seems more like a diversionary tactic. It is a school of mediocrity that teaches us how to get close to the fire of God's pure passion without getting burnt. The trick is to get just close enough to be warmed by the fire. That's lukewarmness.[4]

Such Catholics as Greeley and McNamara believe that the Catholic charismatic movement is alien to Catholicism, an emotional outpouring that is a false spirituality. Certainly there was little in nineteenth- and twentieth-century U.S. Catholicism to indicate that Pentecostalism would take root in the Church, and that by the end of the 1970s there would be hundreds of thousands of Catholic charismatics meeting in hundreds of prayer groups throughout the country.

However, one should recall that certain aspects of the Catholic charismatic movement were evident in preconciliar U.S. Catholicism. Novenas were often marked by spiritual enthusiasm. Healing has always been part of the U.S. Catholic experience— whether in such experiences as Lourdes and Fatima, in such rituals as the blessing of throats on the Feast of St. Blaise, or in the context of a public or private novena. The difference in the contemporary charismatic movement is that such manifestations of the Holy Spirit are much more an integral part of the religious experience.

In November 1968, the National Conference of Catholic Bishops recommended that a formal study of the movement be made by its Committee on Doctrine. A year later the Committee made its report, in which it declared the movement to be theologically sound, with a strong biblical basis. The most prudent way to judge the movement, the report continues, is to observe its effects:

> There are many indications that this participation leads to a better understanding of the role the Christian plays in the Church. Many have experienced progress in their spiritual life. They are attracted to the reading of the scriptures and a deeper understanding of their faith. They seem to grow in their attachment to certain established doctrinal patterns such as devotion to the real presence and the rosary.[5]

It was too soon, the Committee declared, to draw a definite conclusion. Nevertheless, it was recommended that the movement "not be inhibited but allowed to develop," with appropriate pastoral supervision.

The decade that followed this report witnessed not only a rapid growth of Catholic charismatics among the laity, but also among priests, male and female religious, and even a few bishops.

The modern Pentecostal movement has many forerunners, among whom the Irvingites in England during the 1830s were perhaps the most significant. The modern movement, however, originated in the late nineteenth and early twentieth centuries. It seems to have welled up more or less simultaneously and independently in various parts of the world, notably Armenia, Wales, India, and the southern and western United States. Pentecostalism was not a function of any one denomination, although in the United States the Holiness churches had a special importance in preparing the way for it. The mainstream can be dated from New Year's Day 1901. In Charles Parham's Bible school in Topeka, Kansas, a devout prayer service had been held on New Year's Eve to prepare for the coming year. On New Year's Day itself, the "presence of the Lord" was still there, "stilling hearts to wait upon him for greater things," according to Miss Agnes Ozman, one of the students. She felt impelled to ask Parham to lay his hands on her head, as was done in the New Testament, so that she might receive the gift of the Holy

Spirit. When this was done, she underwent a remarkable spiritual experience. "It was as though rivers of living waters were proceeding from my inmost being," she later declared. She began to pray in strange tongues.[6]

Pentecostalism spread erratically and unobtrusively through the Southwest during the next few years. It flared up in Los Angeles in 1906. But those who adhered to Pentecostalism were for the most part driven out of the established churches by ridicule, persecution, or excommunication. As a consequence, they were led to congregate together in new churches and denominations, which are usually categorized as Pentecostal.

During the 1950s, Pentecostalism entered into a new phase, as the charisms began to be received by members of established churches who refused to withdraw and join Pentecostal denominations, but instead remained in the churches to which they already belonged. This phenomenon, called "Neo-Pentecostalism," became one of the major developments in U.S. Protestantism during the 1960s.

Thus, it was perhaps inevitable that the Pentecostal movement should also appear within the Roman Catholic Church. Nevertheless, when it occurred it astounded most observers. The majority of Catholics have either not taken the Pentecostals seriously or have recoiled from the emotionalism and fanaticism which seemed to be associated with them. No one, therefore, was prepared for the ready acceptance which Pentecostal spirituality was accorded once it had gotten a start in the Catholic Church. It has spread far more rapidly there than in any other of the established churches, and the opposition to it has been much less intransigent.

What is the essence of Pentecostal spirituality and what are its contemporary characteristics in U.S. Catholicism? The Pentecostal experience in Christianity is rooted in the role of the Holy Spirit as delineated in the Gospels and in the events of Pentecost. The Acts of the Apostles describes these events: .

When Pentecost day came around, they had all met in one room, when suddenly they heard what sounded like a powerful wind from heaven, the noise of which filled the entire house in which they were sitting; and something appeared to them that seemed like tongues of fire; these separated and came to rest on the head of each of them. They were all filled with the Holy Spirit, and began to speak foreign languages as the Spirit gave them the gift of speech.[7]

The "baptism in the Holy Spirit" gave the assembled followers of Jesus a courage to bear witness and to preach His message, which they had hitherto lacked. It also imparted to them a special gift, or charism, of being able to speak in languages (or tongues) not known to them.

A quarter of a century after Pentecost the apostle Paul took up the matter of charisms as experienced by the church in Corinth:

One may have the gift of preaching with wisdom given him by the Spirit; another may have the gift of preaching instruction given him by the same Spirit; and another the gift of faith given by the same Spirit; another again the gift of healing through this one Spirit; one, the power of miracles; another prophecy; another the gift of recognizing spirits; another the gift of tongues and another the ability to interpret them.[8]

Pentecostalism, then, is rooted in the New Testament consciousness of the Holy Spirit and in the extraordinary manifestation of the Spirit. As such it is intensely biblical, and Scripture plays a major role in the Catholic charismatic experience in a way that it has not done in Catholicism during the past few centuries. The foremost theologian of the Catholic charismatic movement, Berkeley Jesuit Donald Gelpi, suggests a reason for this:

... Both the preoccupations of theological polemics and the limitations of positivistic theological method have focused most of the Catholic community's attention on other issues and questions. It is clear, for instance, that Catholic theology is still in the process of reappropriating its biblical heritage. To be sure, it never really denied that heritage, but in the post-Reformation debates about the normative character of Scripture and tradition, theologians became preoccupied almost to excess with demonstrating the scriptural basis for post-biblical theological concepts. In the process, Scripture tended to be overlooked as a theological resource in its own right.[9]

The concept of "baptism in the Holy Spirit," so fundamental to the Pentecostal experience (including the Catholic charismatic movement), has created some theological difficulties. This "born again" facet of Pentecostalism has been interpreted by some Pentecostal groups as being a sacrament. For Catholics, however, "baptism in the Holy Spirit" is understood not to be a sacrament. Therefore, they feel it does not express as fully as the sacraments the historical, ecclesiastical, and incarnational aspects of the redemption process. For Catholic charismatics, "baptism in the Holy Spirit" is a two-dimensional process—that of the person seeking "baptism in the Holy Spirit" and the response of God. Essentially, then, it is a prayer of petition, which presupposes that the individual in question has decided to break with sin and truly desires to imitate Christ, that he or she has achieved sufficient freedom and detachment of heart to be willing to follow wherever God is leading, and that the petitioner is seriously committed to the task of learning docility to the Spirit of Christ through regular prayer. The petitioner is also completely receptive to whatever gifts the Spirit may choose to give him or her.

The gifts that God may give to the person who has been "baptized in the Holy Spirit," according to charismatics, can include the gift of tongues (or glossolalia), the gift of prophecy, the gift of visions, and the gift of healing. And, while these gifts, particularly that of speaking in tongues, are the most visible and the most discussed by noncharismatics, Catholic charismatics are careful to point out that they are not essential to charismatic spirituality. God may or may not bestow these gifts upon an individual; and possessing them is not a criterion of one's holiness.

The question has frequently arisen as to why these gifts are being manifested in the twentieth century after having disappeared from the Church for so long. St. Augustine had proposed the theory that certain charismatic gifts, among them the gift of tongues, were granted by the Spirit to the apostolic community in order to ensure the establishment of the Christian Church. But once that purpose was achieved, these gifts were withdrawn and replaced by others. This theory is beyond either conclusive proof or conclusive refutation. And, following St. Augustine's own theoretical basis, one cannot therefore conclude that the Holy Spirit is incapable of bestowing the same gifts again, should an historical need for them arise.[10]

It is difficult to describe the structures of the Catholic charismatic movement in the United States today. The experience varies quite dramatically. From a community of Benedictines, composed of both men and women, at Our Lady of Guadalupe Abbey in Pecos, New Mexico; to the large covenant communities in Ann Arbor, Michigan, and South Bend, Indiana; to the prayer meetings at Most Holy Redeemer Center in Oakland, California, Catholic charismatics lead very diverse lives.

The covenant community is probably the most intense. Such communities are generally formed because a group wishes to orient their lives, both individually and collectively, around the central factor of their relationship to God. Thus, they are not unlike the historical monastic communities, religious orders, and even religiously-based utopian communities.

Typically, the group purchases or rents a large house, lives together, and conducts their liturgical and prayer services within that house. Marrieds, unmarrieds, and children all live some form of common life; and, aside from outside work experience, the community forms the basis for one's day-to-day existence.

It is also possible to have a covenant community which does not live together. Such communities are more akin to the conventional parish: members assemble one or more times a week for prayer and worship, but they live apart.

There are also noncovenant groups that assemble in private homes or other facilities for prayer meetings. This is done on a voluntary basis—without the formality of a covenant or commitment to guidelines and rules.

The intensity of the spiritual life of Catholic charismatics in the United States, however, has not been without its problems within the institutional structure of the U.S. Catholic Church. Despite the increased acceptance of the charismatic movement by U.S. Catholic bishops and priests, tensions have arisen. Some of these problems are attributable to the ecumenical aspects of the charismatic movement. Other difficulties stem from some charismatics' comprehension of the sacramental life of the Church in their religious lives. And still other problems revolve around the leadership and rules of certain charismatic communities.

One is tempted to see such problems in their historical context—as being part of the tradition of groups of spiritual "enthusiasts" which have either been excommunicated by the Church or assimilated within its structures.[11] The earliest case in Christianity of a Pentecostal movement being "thrown out" of the Church was that of Montanus and his followers during the latter half of the third century. It seems that the sectarian and heretical tendency developed among the Montanists to such an extent that they came to see their extraordinary gifts as the only authentic gifts of the Spirit, while expecting a second coming of Jesus very soon. They considered as imperfect all Christians who did not experience the same gifts and submit to radical asceticism; and they rejected the regular hierarchy of the Church as not sufficiently spiritual.[12]

There are Catholics who view many U.S. Catholic charismatics as being capable of becoming the new Montanists. One example of this illustrates the problem of ecumenism and the sacramental life of the Church within the charismatic movement. A large covenant community at Loyola University in Los Angeles had decided that it wouldn't celebrate the liturgy any longer: that the spontaneous prayer and "manifestations of the Spirit" were sufficient. As a result, this group was no longer allowed to meet at Loyola University.

A variation of this problem arises when non-Catholic Pentecostals participate in Catholic charismatic gatherings. If these prayer meetings include the liturgy, Catholic charismatics are loathe not to invite their non-Catholic brethren to partake in Communion—even though this is currently forbidden by ecclesiastical laws.

The question of the leadership of various charismatic communities also evokes a nervous reaction on the part of Catholic bishops and priests. The examples of the Rev. Jim Jones and the Peoples Temple, the Unification Church, and other religious groups are too near for Catholic leaders not to fear similar experiences on the part of some Catholic charismatic communities. Certain of these communities, reportedly, have set up a rigid authoritarian structure that controls virtually every aspect of the lives of their members.[13]

Such tensions and difficulties cannot be taken lightly by the institutional Church. Catholic charismatics intruded into a U.S. Catholicism already rent by dissensions, in which priests, nuns, and brothers were leaving in unprecedented numbers, in which vocations to the priesthood and to the religious orders were falling off drastically, and in which participation in the liturgical and sacramental life of the Church on the part of the laity had slumped. What many Catholics considered to be "un-Catholic" or a manifestation of "the lunatic fringe of Protestantism"—Pentecostalism—now became part of the Catholic Church in the United States—and a rapidly growing one at that. The initial concern and antagonism of Catholic bishops and priests and the suspicion of many of the laity soon gave way to a "wait-and-see" tolerance and then acceptance, a feeling that as long as the charismatic experience was integrated into the existing doctrinal, sacramental, and hierarchical structure of the Church, there need be few problems with the alien qualities of the movement.

However, religious movements founded upon an individual "inner light" are always regarded with suspicion. The traditional anarchical tendencies of these movements generally confront the established structures of institutional churches. Such a confrontation now appears to be developing between one segment of the Catholic charismatic movement and the institutional Church, and although it is too early to predict the outcome, it is likely that Catholic charismatic communities that cut themselves off from the institutional Church will soon become small, ingrown sects that will, in time, wither away.

On the other hand, it appears that Catholic Pentecostalism is going to become an increasingly integrated and permanent part of the U.S. Catholic Church. Institutional structures and forms are already accommodating to this aspect of religious pluralism: for example, large charismatic communities are being constituted as parishes and bishops are paying more attention to pastoral coordination with charismatic groups in their dioceses.

That the explosive growth of Pentecostalism should have occurred within the U.S. Catholic Church when it did should not surprise anyone. There has been a continual tradition of "enthusiasm" within the Church; and the U.S. religious experience during the 1960s and 1970s has tended away from the secularist and the cerebral (perhaps most visible in Unitarianism) towards what can be described as an affective experience (as witnessed by "fundamentalism"). The contraction of "ghetto Catholicism" during the 1950s and 1960s and the openness to new modes of religious experience following the Second Vatican Council also provided conditions favorable to the Pentecostal experience in U.S. Catholicism.

Nor can one overlook other aspects of contemporary U.S. life as fostering a fertile ambience for the growth of the Catholic charismatic movement. The weariness with the social explosions of the 1960s and early 1970s, the reaction against the anonymity of the industrial and technological expansion of the post-World War II period, and the sense of collapsed community that has particularly marked the urban experience areas are all factors that helped to spark the charismatic movement. After all, one of the principal characteristics of charismatic groups is that of community—whether in those covenant communities that form as living together groups or in more informal prayer groups. These groups all bear the characteristics of a type of extended family.

Postconciliar Catholicism also produced conditions that stimulated the growth of Catholic Pentecostalism. Many Catholics found the changes following the Second Vatican Council drastic and confusing. They found the revamped liturgy dull and unsatisfying; and they were distressed by the split in the Church between liberals and conservatives. This split, with its resulting dissensions, seemed to overlook prayer and spirituality in order to concentrate on abstruse theological concepts and the minutiae of political squabbling. The parish had died as both a nurturing community and as a meaningful source of the spiritual augmentation of Catholics. Thus the conditions were ripe for both a new community experience and a new mode of spiritual expression.

Catholic charismatics frequently have been accused of a lack of social involvement; and the writings and speeches of movement leaders have often reflected one side or the other of this problem. Some have discussed the necessity of personal, internal renewal before becoming involved in social action. Others have dealt with this problem in terms of organizational considerations: that the charismatic movement is still too new and too fragile to become involved in social action; and to do so would cause strife and dissension. Seen in perspective, however, the question can be discussed in terms of the age-old tension between action and contemplation, in the paradox of "the desert and the city."

The question is often asked as to what will be the long-term status of Catholic charismatics in the U.S. Catholic Church. This kind of speculation is always hazardous. As the charismatic movement burst unexpectedly upon the Church in the first place, one should be wary of indulging in forecasting the future of the movement. One view is that the charismatic movement will be absorbed into the Church—a view which Jesuit sociologist Joseph Fichter records as follows:

> The contemporary charismatic movement is seen as a type of spiritual force for Church renewal that will lose its identity as it becomes fully absorbed into the whole of Catholicism. No less a personage than Cardinal Suenens has predicted that Catholic pentecostalism "will disappear as a movement as quickly as possible and enter into the blood and life of the Church. Once the river gets to the sea you don't speak of the river any more." George Martin points out that "the goal is a charismatically renewed Church, not a separate pentecostal organization for people who go for that sort of thing." Such spokesmen suggest parallels with the once flourishing biblical and liturgical movements which are no longer structurally identifiable within the Catholic Church because their purposes have been accomplished.[14]

This theory (which Fichter puts forth but does not advocate) is certainly a strong possibility. It is also possible, however, that the Catholic charismatic movement will continue to be a spiritual movement within a pluralistic Church, and that the institutional Church will accommodate its structures to include charismatic groups as a parallel to its parish organization.

The experience of a Catholic charismatic meeting—whether a prayer meeting or a liturgical celebration—is an unusual one for a Catholic who has only witnessed the traditional liturgical or devotional events in most Catholic parishes. Prayer group members and strangers alike are warmly greeted upon entering the home, church, or other facility where a charismatic group has gathered. Warm embraces, joyful smiles, friendly greetings, and mutual encouragement all illustrate the close and friendly relationships that exist within the local prayer group—and which are extended to those attending for the first time. When the Eucharist is celebrated at the meetings, the members join hands during the recitation of the Lord's Prayer and they exchange the Kiss of Peace in a manner that bespeaks their spiritual solidarity. For contrast, one need merely observe the relatively aloof way in which this ritual is performed at Sunday mass in many parish churches.

One is also struck by the spontaneity and emotionalism of the charismatic prayer meeting and liturgical service. Personal testimonies of how someone has been "touched by God," and how that conversion has made a difference in his or her life, frequent reading of the Scriptures (including opening the Bible at random and reading the first passage that strikes the eye), the fervent singing of hymns, usually accompanied by guitars, the punctuation of all that is going on with frequent cries of "Praise the Lord" and "Alleleuia," and, of course, those times when the gathering will break forth in tongues—a harmonious blending of sounds that seems to have a life of its own—are all features of a Catholic charismatic meeting.

Joseph Fichter indicates the amazement of noncharismatic Catholics when he writes:

> The second surprise is that this spontaneous and informal spiritual movement should take hold within a hierarchical, stylized, liturgical and sacramental system like Catholicism. Emotional expressions of religious had long ago been tamed, brought under control, or at least conventionalized in the Catholic Church,

particularly in the Irish-Anglo version that is predominant in the United States. There was no room for outbursts of spiritual enthusiasm, spontaneous prayer and prophecy, speaking in tongues, handclapping, or the joyful singing of hymns. One would have expected to witness these activities in a revivalist tent full of Holy Rollers, but not in a Catholic Church.[15]

Healing is another facet of the Catholic charismatic meeting that strikes the noncharismatic as a transplant from Protestant revivalism. The once scoffed-at activities of the faith healer are now an essential aspect of Catholic charismatic meetings. Elmer Gantry has come to the Catholic Church, one is tempted to say. And, indeed, Catholic charismatics hold in admiration well-known Protestant healers like Kathryn Kuhlman, Oral Roberts, Agnes Sanford, and Ruth Carter Stapleton.

Three principal types of healing are practiced in Catholic charismatic gatherings: the first is the conversion event itself, which intensifies the repentence for sin; the second is the inner healing of memories, which helps to resolve emotional problems; the third is the actual curing of physical illness and ailments.

The latter aspect of healing is, of course, the most controversial. In one group, a woman complains of having a migraine headache. Several men and women gather around her, place their hands on her, and pray. After several moments, the woman smiles. The migraine headache is gone. Confessions, testimonies, and even medical records are offered by many charismatics as evidence of the efficacy of the healing ministry. One man tells how he has been cured of alcoholism; many claim cures from the ravages of cancer; others offer proof in the form of x-rays and confirmation from physicians that bone deformities have been cured.

The healing ministry in the Catholic charismatic movement is seen as an example of the power of faith in God. No healer claims to be more than an instrument in the hands of the Lord, but all insist that both the healer and the sick person must have complete faith in God before a miraculous cure can be anticipated. Fichter writes:

> The believer does not question the power of God to heal sickness. He firmly believes that the person who asks in the name of

Jesus for a healing, either for himself or for others, can obtain the answer to his petition. To believe that God can heal is not the same as to possess the charism of healing. In the language of the charismatic renewal, the pentecostal Catholic receives the charism of healing through the baptism of the Holy Spirit, and this means that God's healing power is available to him whether or not he becomes a recognized minister of healing.[16]

An unexpected movement in the U.S. Catholic Church, and one which is less than a decade and a half old, is difficult to assess. One has to differentiate between a theological evaluation of the Catholic charismatic movement and a consideration of its future place in the institutional Church. Further, one has to determine whether the movement of charismatic renewal within the U.S. Catholic Church does not partake of essentially anarchical tendencies, compounded by separatism, which will eventually preclude its becoming part of the mainstream of U.S. Catholic life.

Despite the strictures of writers such as William McNamara, Andrew Greeley, and others, the Catholic charismatic movement has received the approbation of the U.S. hierarchy. And most Catholic theologians seem to agree that Catholic Pentecostalism is in accordance with the doctrines of the Church. But this official *nihil obstat* does not answer certain fundamental questions.

These questions, which are more sociological in nature than theological, revolve around the development of the organization and structures of the Catholic charismatic movement and their relationship to the institutional Church in the United States as a whole. Can a very different spiritual expression exist within that Church? And, if it can, how will the movement of charismatic renewal influence U.S. Catholicism and in turn be influenced by the mainstream of the traditional Church? Will tendencies toward anticlericalism, rigid authoritarian leadership within some covenant communities, and a relinquishment of the sacramental life of the Church expand? Will the influence of Protestant Pentecostalism on Catholic charismatics broaden?

Thus far, the Catholic charismatic movement has been the most visible and discernible experience of spiritual renewal in U.S. Catholicism following the Second Vatican Council. The decade and more of conflict within the Church following the council left a sense of disillusion and perplexity and a spiritual void that to some extent has been filled by the Catholic charismatic movement. It has provided a vital role in the confusing aftermath of the council. But, just as Pentecostalism continues to be a minority movement within the Protestant churches, it is to be expected that the charismatic movement will be a minority experience within the U.S. Catholic Church. It remains to be seen, however, whether Catholic charismatics will provide the leaven for a "new Pentecost" within the Church.

The medium-sized dining room on the mezzanine of the Hotel San Franciscan is jammed by 7:30 on this Sunday morning. A varied assortment of individuals sit and stand, waiting for mass to begin: some older men and women, rosary beads clutched in their hands, others who are middle-aged, mostly women, and some young men, faintly effete in their bearing. At 8 A.M. a priest wearing a biretta, holding in his hands a covered chalice, enters from the back of the room. Upon the signal of a clanging bell those in the room stand as the priest, preceded by two altar boys, goes to the improvised altar, removes his biretta and hands it to the altar boy to his right. The trio genuflects, and the priest places the chalice on the center of the altar. He then returns and stands at the foot of the altar. The altar boys and the congregation kneel.

"In nomine Patris, Filii, et Spiritu Sancti," begins the priest. "Introibo ad altare Dei."

"Ad Deum qui laetificat juventutem meum," respond the altar boys.

It is the beginning of the Tridentine mass. But, the observer realizes, while this might have been one of countless such masses celebrated on one of countless Sundays and weekdays before the mid-1960s, the year is 1978. The Tridentine mass has been abolished as the result of the liturgical changes which occurred following the Second Vatican Council.

It is the Feast of St. Joan of Arc; and when the priest begins his sermon, it is evident what is taking place. He excoriates the Second Vatican Council, accuses the pope of allowing the Church to be "Protestantized," and calls for the Church to come back to its traditional beliefs and devotions. "Let us save the Church as

Joan of Arc saved France," he concludes. The members of the congregation nod in agreement.

Following benediction at the conclusion of the mass, a couple approaches me and asks, "Have you been to mass here before?"

"No," I reply, "this is my first time."

"Are you a Catholic?"

"Yes, I am."

"Don't you just hate what those heretics did at the so-called Vatican Council? They took away the Latin mass that has been in the Church for more than a thousand years. And they've done away with devotion to the Blessed Mother. They've turned the Catholic Church Protestant."

I nod politely, not wishing to become entangled in a theological discussion with these representatives of the "remnant of Israel," and promise that I will be back.

The mass at the Hotel San Franciscan is representative of masses celebrated weekly in cities throughout the United States under the auspices of various groups who have rejected the changes, reforms, and renewal of the Second Vatican Council: among them, the Catholic Traditionalist Movement, sparked by Father Gommar De Pauw, a priest of the Archdiocese of Baltimore, in the mid-1960s; the Legion of Mary; and the followers of Archbishop Marcel Lefebvre.

These groups contend that the council fathers at the Second Vatican Council and those who subsequently implemented the council's actions were guilty of leading the Church into heresy, that they were defying God's intentions for the Church. It was similar to the periodic lapses of Israel into idolatry: and these groups were playing the role of Old Testament prophets in bringing the Church back to its true course.

The attraction of this traditionalist movement, which in earlier days would have been labelled "schismatic" and read out of the Church, seems to have been primarily for older Catholics who could not or would not adapt to the changes brought about by the Second Vatican Council. The age-old liturgy, devotions, and exclusivity of the Church had brought them solace throughout their lives; and now, in the midst of a society that seemed chaotic—with burnings, demonstrations, and urban crime—the

Church had changed. Not only did it change the liturgy, de-emphasized devotion to Mary and the saints, and hold "ecumenical" conversations with Protestant churches, but nuns were wearing what everyone else wore and priests were leaving the priesthood to get married.

Such goings-on were inconceivable to those who had been nurtured on the idea that priests were almost godlike and that nuns were angelic creatures. That priests and nuns were leaving their vocations in record numbers, that they were donning street clothes and marching in antiwar and civil rights demonstrations, and that they were getting married were surely signs that God had turned His face from this heretical Church.

But the traditionalist movement never caught on in U.S. Catholicism. The malaise that overcame the U.S. Church in the 1960s and 1970s did not translate itself into a widespread conservative movement that essentially separated itself from the official Church. Catholics may have ceased going to church, some joined other churches, and others sought for a relationship to the Church of their past by retaining the traditional devotional practices of the preconciliar Church; but very few became actively involved in any of the rear-guard traditionalist groups.

These groups now seem to be dying out. Unable to recruit Catholics in any substantial numbers, and with no prospect of doing so in the future, they form today an exotic religious movement—its adherents older and older, meeting in tiny enclaves.

But if those conservatives who have cut themselves off from the official Church face eventual extinction, this is not true of numerous Catholics who are rediscovering a new orthodoxy within U.S. Catholicism. This movement, which I call neo-orthodoxy, has numerous manifestations. It is today one of the most vital movements in U.S. Catholicism.

Labels are always difficult to compose. "Conservative" brings forth one image, "liberal" another. The word "orthodox" is usually associated with "conservative," and therefore those whom we call "orthodox" will be labeled by many "conservative" or "reactionary." That labels frequently are simple ways of defining complex realities should be obvious to everyone. In religious matters, such complexities, and the inadequacy of labels, are even more obvious. While it is true historically and currently that many who are orthodox theologically are conservative politically, it is also true, that one can be orthodox theologically and liberal politically. The prime example in U.S. Catholicism of such diverse positions is Dorothy Day. Ms. Day represented a pioneering, minuscule movement in U.S. Catholicism that saw Catholicism as extending to pacificism and aggressive social justice. At the same time she and her followers remained doctrinally quite orthodox.

(There are many charming stories about this seeming dichotomy in Dorothy Day's views. According to one such account, after Father Daniel Berrigan had finished saying mass at the Catholic Worker house in New York, leaving numerous tiny particles of the bread which he had consecrated for the Eucharist, Ms. Day was quite concerned that these unconsumed remnants of the Host would be thrown out, desecrated. She proceeded to sweep up every particle that she could find in order that this would not happen, emulating what priests had traditionally done with crumbs remaining from the Host.)

This should not be seen as paradoxical: for there need not be a dichotomy between an orthodox faith and various interpretations of that orthodoxy—all of which might be valid. Avery Dulles and Rosemary Ruether might disagree on theological interpretations of Catholic beliefs; but is one orthodox and the other not?

What I call neo-orthodoxy might better be called neo-traditionalism or neo-conservatism—a movement similar to those ultramontane tendencies that became part of European Catholicism during the nineteenth century. For at the heart of the neo-orthodox movement in U.S. Catholicism is a return to traditional beliefs and practices and a greater acceptance of the historical Catholic concept of the teaching *magisterium* of the Church. A great deal of this movement is rooted in the cultural *ethos* of present-day Western society—a move away from the innovative energies of the 1960s and early 1970s towards greater stability. This is, of course, part of the historical cyclical process that alternates between rapid, compressed change and the times when that change is absorbed and assimilated. The current age is one of those times of assimilation, one which seeks certainty rather than experimentation, stability rather than change.

The nascent movement of neo-orthodoxy in U.S. Catholicism mirrors this prevailing mood; and the manifestations of the movement center around a search of the past to provide coherence for the present and meaning for the future. Rarely do Catholics any longer extol the secular, "the world," as being of supreme relevance to their religious faith. It is inconceivable today that a Sister Jacqueline Grennan, then president of Webster College (now Mrs. Wechsler, president of Hunter College in New York), would talk about the large anonymous force for good to be found in corporations like Monsanto or would compare the inaugural address of John F. Kennedy to a "new Pentecost." No, the adulation of the secular, with its attendant celebration of power, technology, and the efficient use of resources to accomplish anything, collapsed with Vietnam, the Great Society, and Watergate. And if the secular did not provide the answer to U.S. Catholicism, neither did the strident speculations of the "new theology." In the late 1970s it became evident that even if one conceded that the new theologians gave light, they did not nourish; if their speculations caused one to think more clearly about the doctrines of Catholicism, they nevertheless seemed to lead nowhere. The lessons of liberal Protestantism loomed for all to see: doctrines constantly modified and made palatable to each succeeding age are without followers.

It is too early to know what form neo-orthodoxy in U.S. Catholicism will take. At this point there is much evidence that it resembles the *Jubilee* Catholicism of the 1950s and early 1960s. The revival of interest in monasticism is certainly an indication of this aspect of U.S. Catholicism. More than a decade after his death in 1968, the Trappist monk Thomas Merton exerts an influence that exceeds even that which he wielded following publication of his best-selling autobiography, *Seven Storey Mountain*, in the 1950s. His books are being reprinted, and sell quite well. Writings, unpublished during his lifetime, are being collected and published. Three or four new biographies are being readied. Merton institutes and conferences are springing up throughout the United States.

The revival of interest in Thomas Merton is being reflected in the numbers of those applying to enter the most rigorous of Catholic monasteries (such as Merton's own Cistercian, or Trappist, order). Not since the 1950s and early 1960s have there been so many applicants to U.S. monasteries.

It also appears that U.S. monasticism is having an effect on lay Catholic piety. Large numbers are flocking to monasteries for retreats; and monastic spirituality is once again influencing the spiritual life of laypersons.

Neo-orthodoxy is further being manifested in vocations to religious orders. While the key word following Vatican II was "modernization," the guiding concept today seems to be tradition. Those religious orders that have most modernized in matters of dress, apostolate, and way of life are paradoxically those which have become least successful in recruiting new members (for example, the Religious of the Sacred Heart of Jesus, which retained the practices and customs of its eighteenth-century French beginnings until its transformation in the 1960s into a very liberal, almost "hip," congregation). Many of these religious orders are faced with dwindling numbers and the eventuality that they will become extinct. On the other hand, those orders, particularly of women, which have retained most of the traditional characteristics of religious life are the most successful in attracting new vocations. "If I wanted to live in an apartment, do my own thing, wear normal lay clothes, and date men, I could do that just as easily as a laywoman," one woman who had recently entered such a traditional convent told me.

These manifestations of a return to more traditional religious patterns in contemporary U.S. Catholicism are evidenced in the St. Ignatius Institute at the University of San Francisco, a Jesuit-operated university. The St. Ignatius Institute illustrates both the evidence of neo-orthodoxy among many Catholic college students and the continuing divisions within U.S. Catholicism. Set up as the brainchild of Father Joseph Fessio, a young, energetic Jesuit, the Institute was developed to admit those students, Catholic or non-Catholic, who wished to focus on a more humanistically integrated liberal arts education and who wished Catholic theology to be a part of that education.

Fessio, a conservative theologically, has based the Institute on the traditional teaching authority of the Church as the foundation for the study of theology, and although the students in the St. Ignatius Institute are not required to attend any religious ceremony or to partake in any devotion, they early began to gather together for such purposes. Many attend daily mass together. The recitation of the rosary and the nocturnal adoration of the Blessed Sacrament devotion have become popular. Some of the students in the Institute meet to read the Divine Office each day.

Are the students of the St. Ignatius Institute a symbol of the future of the U.S. Catholic Church? Do they reflect a trend which will mark the Church in the 1980s? Probably. The excesses of protest that marked the U.S. Church in the second half of the 1960s and the early 1970s have no hold on these students nor on most of the young Catholics in the country today. Radical theological speculations, so prevalent during the same period, have little interest for them. They are more interested in the works of Teresa of Avila than those of Rosemary Ruether, the life of Thomas More rather than that of Charles Davis. These students don't see their involvement with the St. Ignatius Institute as a preconciliar throwback nor as a conservative rear-guard action. Instead, they believe that they are learning a tradition which is applicable to their contemporary world: the assimilation of the past into the present.

The students of the Institute are, of course, part of a broader movement in the United States—and part of a broader movement in the contemporary religious life of the nation. Young men and women, for the past several years, have been flocking to conservative churches and to a wide array of spiritual communities. It is no surprise that this conservative, orthodox trend is affecting U.S. Catholics as well. This has become a time for healing, for assimilating the ferment that has occurred during the past fifteen years, and for discovering the nature of union with God within the Roman Catholic Church.

# 8/ The Coming of Age of U.S. Catholicism

Should priests be celibate? How can a Catholic use contraception and continue to receive the sacraments? Should women be ordained? What is the U.S. Catholic Church going to do about the decrease in Catholic practice among the young? What about the crisis of authority in the U.S. Church? How is the hierarchy going to revitalize parish life? What will the role of the papacy be in the Church of the future?

The above questions about contemporary U.S. Catholicism, most of which would not have been posed before 1960, indicate a Church in transition. They illustrate the dichotomy between a religious denomination that continues to hold the loyalty of millions of U.S. Catholics, but which faces considerable contraction of members in coming years because of the disaffection of a large (and perhaps growing) number of those under thirty years of age.

Many have written about the need for renewal and reconstruction in U.S. Catholicism since the Second Vatican Council. Most of these accounts fall into one of two categories: first, abstract theological speculations that have no relevance to the spiritual needs of the mass of U.S. Catholics; and second, suggestions tied to one small aspect of a possible Catholic renewal. While both of these categories contribute somewhat to the Catholic mosaic of revitalization, a clear definition of what it means to be a Catholic and a corresponding implementation of that sense of Catholicism are probably not going to spring from the detached teachings of theologians, nor from the "nuts and bolts" suggestions of those who contribute to the fields of catechetics, liberation theology, or other limited areas of the Catholic religious experience. (This statement is not meant to denigrate the validity of these areas in the Christian experience nor the value of those who contribute to them. Rather, I wish to indicate that the Christian commitment is infinitely more powerful than the sum of such considerations as what kind of filmstrips to show Confirmation classes or the sometimes smug, indignant accusations of liberation theologians.)

Renewal and reconstruction must come from touching that wellspring of latent spiritual force in U.S. Catholicism and allowing it to flow into the totality of life in the Church. To accomplish this, the present leadership of the U.S. Catholic Church must be charged with the importance of the Church's mission and fulfill its duties as spiritual leaders of the "people of God."

An example of such a radical concept of leadership is exemplified by the charismatic pastor of a fundamentalist church in Santa Rosa, California. The church is noted for the throngs that crowd into its large structure each Sunday. Many of its worshipers are from so-called mainline Protestant denominations or are disaffected Catholics. The congregation bears many of the earmarks of an extended family, a close-knit community similar to what the Christian churches must have been like in the first century of Christianity.

The church in Santa Rosa is also known for the large sums of money collected from its members, and for the large contributions it makes to foreign missionary activities, and to the feeding, clothing, and housing of the poor in its own area. In discussing this with two friends of mine, both Episcopalians, one said, "I'll have to go up there to get some pointers for my church's stewardship program." The other responded, "You've got it backwards. What that pastor has done is to preach the love of Jesus so that the people of the church open their pocketbooks of their own accord in order to help preach that love around the world and to help their fellow human beings."

It is easy to dismiss this church as being fundamentalist or revivalist, and to raise the specter of an unsophisticated religious phenomenon. I question, however, whether living the revolutionary message of the Gospels is much different from this experience.

Catholic spirituality is rooted in a three-fold individual response to the Gospel, which can be characterized by the concepts of community, discipleship, and mission. This three-fold response is the key to the reconstruction of the U.S. Catholic Church. Although the world is constantly changing, although humanity's response to the One God may be inadequate, although Revelation needs to be appropriated anew, and although human nature is often baffling, the need for this response to the Gospel is unchanging.

"Community" means both the ecclesial community and the living community. "Discipleship" centers around what has been called "saying yes to Christ," expressing one's love for Him, and attaining union with God. Thus the elements of prayer and worship are essential to the component of discipleship—not only individually, but also communally. "Mission" has traditionally called for the element of apostleship, of evangelization.

This three-fold response to the Gospel, so manifest in the Church depicted in the *Acts of the Apostles*, remains today the basis for Christianity—and must be the basis for the reconstruction of the U.S. Catholic Church in the 1980s. This chapter will attempt to describe a U.S. Catholicism come of age.

In the early 1970s, theologian David J. O'Brien wrote a passage that rang with hope, amidst a disordered, outraged nation and a confused U.S. Catholic Church:

> To those who still think in the categories of the 1930s or the 1950s the situation is depressing; to those who long for liberation to a brave new world of harmony and freedom it is exhilarating. For the rest of us the contemporary situation arouses our hopes while it nourishes our fears; it promises a better church and a better world even as the threat of spiritual isolation and physical annihilation hover in the background. We are where Christians should be, poised on the razor's edge between present and future, aware of the possibilities for good and evil which open out in front of us. Knowing the reality of sin and the possibility of failure, men must nevertheless push on, rely-

ing on the love of God and their own talents, seeking to build a
Kingdom that will be God's because it will be man's.[1]

The state of balance O'Brien described continues today. In the
future it could result in the "Church of the diaspora" of which
Father Karl Rahner speaks, a mighty lessening of those who are
Catholics, reduced to small groups reminiscent of the early centuries of Christianity; or it could evolve into the spiritual revitalization of the existing Church and the evangelization of those
millions who have not yet accepted Jesus Christ. My own assessment of the times in which we live, so charged with inchoate
spiritual energy, leads me to believe that the time of "diaspora"
is not yet here, and that the future is filled with a variety of possibilities for U.S. Catholicism.

There have been many accounts of what the Catholic Church
of the future should be like. One of the most specific is that of
Dr. James Hitchcock, who could be described as a traditional or
conservative Catholic, in a chapter entitled "The Future of Roman Catholicism" in his recent *Catholicism and Modernity*. In it he
asserts that the first step in the renewal of U.S. Catholicism is
what he calls "the validation of traditional Catholicism." Questions and doubts of conservative Catholics by a liberal minority,
he claims, have resulted in a loss of morale and inner conviction
on the part of many Catholics and have left the Church without
an effective bulwark against indiscriminate innovation.

Hitchcock's antidote against this alienation and indiscriminate
innovation is contained in a four-point program which calls for
a sacral liturgy, which incorporates both "small group" Eucha-
rists and a community celebration of the solemn, complete liturgy of the Church; orthodox catechetics, a solid grounding in
doctrine; clarity of doctrine, asserted by firm and unambiguous
guidance concerning the distinction between official Church
doctrine and mere opinion; and moral firmness. Those who pick
and choose among the Church's doctrines and conceive for
themselves a role of combative dissent in the Church should not
be compromised with, for such a strategy will be fatal and un-
productive. Hitchcock goes on to discuss such topics as "the recovery of zeal," "the revitalization of institutions within the

Church," "the recovery of a sense of social order," and "new ecumenical directions."

Hitchcock's plan for recovery can be described as the traditionalist or conservative position: it looks to the past as the corrective norm for the future. He argues not for a return to the preconciliar Church, but for correctives to many unwarranted innovations that became prevalent during and after the Second Vatican Council and for the traditional Catholic viewpoint with regard to the teaching authority of the Church.

Such a blueprint as Hitchcock's, as well-balanced as it is, need not be examined with regard to such questions as: What is orthodox teaching? What is "firm and unambiguous" teaching? A more basic critique of Hitchcock's position is that the world upon which it is predicated has disappeared. Not just the U.S. Catholic Church has changed during the past two decades; the world has been transformed. Renewal of U.S. Catholicism—its coming of age—must be based upon the essential Christian response to the Gospel, which takes cognizance of this transformed world about us and which does not wish to recreate the conditions that existed for the U.S. Catholic Church in the nineteenth century and first half of the twentieth century.

Let us now examine the following topics of paramount importance in considering the renewal of contemporary U.S. Catholicism.

### The Crisis of Leadership

The U.S. Catholic Church early in its history began to resemble the structure and organization of "big business." Perhaps it was no coincidence that the rise of the United States as a major industrial power in the mid-nineteenth century coincided with a century of extraordinary growth for the Church. Bishops and pastors were early faced with administering this growth: building new churches, convents, seminaries, schools. The energies of the men who led the Church were thus largely expended in attending to the physical aspects of the Church's expansion.

In the centralized, authoritarian Church of the nineteenth and early twentieth centuries, those who were considered "safe" often rose to positions of leadership. Among seminarians, the "most promising" were sent to the North American College in Rome, that nurturing institution of future U.S. bishops. After ordination these men were given "staff" jobs; and if they showed administrative ability, learned the intricacies of ecclesiastical politics, and "kept their noses clean," they were consecrated bishops. Such qualities, it is apparent, are those also ascribed to those who survive the process of rising up the corporate ladder. (The selection of Church leaders based on these criteria has not only been true of the nation's bishops, but of the superiors of religious orders as well.)

Not everyone would subscribe to Andrew Greeley's statement that U.S. Catholic bishops are "intellectually, morally and spiritually bankrupt," but most would probably agree with Michael Novak, who states:

> Think for a moment of the average Catholic's relationship to his bishop. When was the last time you yourself received a religious insight from, or shared a Christian experience with, your bishop? Is it not true that your bishop has taught you absolutely *nothing* that is now significant in your daily life as a human being and a Catholic? Bishops simply are not leaders of the spirit.[3]

The spiritual emptiness of Catholic bishops is reflected in the unimaginative leadership of most pastors; and, with a small minority of exceptions, parishes in the U.S. Catholic Church resemble geriatric wards.[4] And the stale "do your own thing" attitude in most religious orders today has blunted the effectiveness of these bodies.

What little lay leadership exists in the U.S. Catholic Church is unfortunately no better than the clerical leadership. Consigned to subordinate roles, laypersons have exercised little influence in the Church. "Safe," unimaginative clerics have co-opted "safe," unimaginative laypersons when sharing of leadership is necessary.

Such a bleak picture of the quality of those who rule and guide the contemporary U.S. Church does not evince much hope that the revitalization of U.S. Catholicism will come from those who traditionally lead the Church. And an organization without competent, imaginative leadership is an organization in trouble. (Most corporations, when the "figures" get bad enough, bring in a new slate of management.) It is to this area—that of providing competent, imaginative, charismatic *spiritual leaders*—that the apostolic delegate in the United States, curial officials, and others responsible for the selection of bishops and superiors of religious orders must address themselves. Or, perhaps, it is time for decentralization of the function of choosing bishops and pastors, allowing instead a greater voice to the communities involved to select their spiritual leaders.

Every aspect of the U.S. Catholic Church is affected by the quality of leadership; and this quality is particularly important for a body that has been traditionally submissive to the will of ecclesiastics. It is unlikely that any renewal and reconstruction of U.S. Catholicism will occur without major changes in the leadership of the U.S. Church.

What about the role of the pope? Will his leadership seriously affect the future of U.S. Catholicism? Certainly the energy and charm of Pope John Paul II, who will probably be in office for the next two decades, will make him a significant factor in the U.S. Catholic Church. The media exposure of his trip to the United States in 1979 and the warmth and goodwill his trip generated certainly indicate that the Pope would like to expand his role in the Church.

However, for all the excitement of John Paul II's trip and for all of his charm, one must conclude that the *real effect* of an expanded papal role in the affairs of the Church will diminish rather than grow. The thrust of the present pope's policy has been towards putting an end to the theological speculation and widespread experimentation that characterized the 1960s and 1970s, rather than providing a charismatic spiritual leadership. For most Catholics, the pope is no longer the awe-inspiring, revered figure he was before the Second Vatican Council. "Roma locuta est, causa finita est" ("Rome has spoken; the matter is closed") is no longer a reality. The attempts at silencing such theologians as Hans Küng and Edward Schillebeeckx may produce a "Vietnam" for the pope and the Roman curia.

Without examining the historical role of the papacy in the Church and without speculating as to its future role, one could safely make the statement that conditions have changed during the past decade and a half. The pope is still capable of influencing the general tone and direction of the Church; but, more and more, it is what develops on the local level that will make its impact on the lives of Catholics. And, although local leadership—the bishops—continues to be determined in Rome, this leadership, if it is going to be effective, must be responsive to the needs of the communities that it serves.

It is in this realm—the appointment of bishops—that the pope will have the greatest influence on the U.S. Catholic Church. It is through this power that the pope will be able to implement his frequent call, "Go to Christ."

## Revitalizing Structures and Organizations

Although the need for restructuring the geographical parish is widely recognized among Catholics, virtually no steps have been taken to alter the traditional concept of the parish—now such an apparently failed vehicle of Catholic spiritual life.

It is obvious to any observer that the future of U.S. Catholicism will revolve around a pluralistic experience. The traditional parish, with its proclivity for uniformity for Catholics living within its geographical boundaries, has not met the diverse needs of its members in recent times—and undoubtedly will not do so in the future. The pastor and his curates, historically concerned in the United States with the ministering of the sacraments and with the economic aspects of parish administration, seem incapable of fulfilling the expanded roles of spiritual guides and facilitators of a Catholic community.

The early Christian experience, with its multiple roles of ministry—bishops, deacons, presbyters, even gravediggers among them—recognized the diverse functions required of ministry and of leaders in the Christian community: to govern, to preach, to teach, to administer the Church's property, to lead the Christian community assembled for worship, and to administer the sacraments. There should be similar efforts today to expand the roles of ministry involved in the leadership of the Church.

For example, every survey shows that the great majority of Catholics are dissatisfied with the quality of sermons preached. Why continue to expect the diocesan clergy, most of whom seem to be incompetent to preach, to deliver all sermons? Why not train individuals called to this ministry, ordain them deacons, and allow them to fulfill this function?

Religious orders have been a factor in Christianity since the early centuries of the Church. Monastic orders and the religious orders and congregations founded for specific functions (e.g., the Dominicans for preaching, the Maryknolls for foreign missionary work) have been part of the mainstream of Catholicism since the dissolution of the Roman Empire. These religious orders have traditionally patterned themselves on monastic ideals: lifetime commitments, the vows of poverty, chastity, and obedience. For fifteen hundred years, the basis for such groups has been the formation of a more or less rigid religious caste. But religious developments in the contemporary United States have illustrated that a more flexible approach to religious communities could be used advantageously by the U.S. Catholic Church.

The increase in numbers flocking to the proliferation of spiritual communities in this country during recent years illustrates the desire of many for some formal religious community. Spiritual communities of Buddhists, Hindus, and Sufis are filled with young former Catholics. So are Christian groups such as the Unification Church and the Holy Order of MANS. Many of these former Catholics claim that they were not able to find in contemporary Catholicism the intense spirituality or the vehicle for the religious life they wished to lead.[5]

Once again, I pose a critical question: Why not spark a sense of the possibility for limited commitments in Catholic spiritual communities? Why not create spiritual communities for Catholics who wish to live a communal life of prayer and service, but who don't wish the traditional, canonical religious life? Such communities have arisen within the Catholic charismatic movement; but Catholic charismatics remain only a small minority of the U.S. Catholic Church.

There has been in the United States during the past several years a great search for new forms of community, reflecting, no doubt, the collapse of conventional marriage and family institutions as well as patterns of mobility. This search for community is frequently matched with a desire for a more intensive spiritual life. It is this combination that perhaps has been at the heart of the traditional monastic experience; and the channeling of this combined search by the U.S. Catholic Church into spiritual communities, using new forms and concepts suited to a contemporary consciousness, could possibly infuse a renewed religious vitality into the U.S. Catholic Church.

The canonically constituted religious orders—the Dominicans, Jesuits, Franciscans, and lesser known religious congregations—are themselves the subject of much scrutiny these days. In few other places in the U.S. Catholic Church does there continue to be so much dissension, lack of focus, and uncertainty. With few exceptions, vocations to these religious orders are minimal. The purpose and labors of most of the orders remain in a state of flux. The conservative-liberal division, and the consequent dissension arising from this division, remains active. The apostolic work of these groups remains blunted as individuals attempt to "find themselves" and their leadership seeks to redefine its purpose.

It appears that those religious orders which have remained most faithful to traditional religious practices, more in tune with a preconciliar spirit, are attracting the most vocations. (This trend is probably part of the rising tendency towards neo-orthodoxy in U.S. Catholicism.)

Despite agonizing reappraisal by most of the religious orders and the constant search for relevant ministries, it will be many years before purposeful vitality returns to these groups; and by then many religious orders will likely be extinct or on the verge of extinction.

Given their present leadership and organizational structures, it is clear that the traditional organizations within the U.S. Catholic Church—the diocese, the parish, the religious orders—are incapable of fostering the renewal and reconstruction of U.S. Catholicism. However, these structures can become catalysts for change. The failure of free-form organizations during the past decade-and-a-half of U.S. Catholicism is all too obvious. *Aggiornamento* should become the literal "opening up" of U.S. Catholic institutions to embrace contemporary forms and requirements, rather than the ironic cause for devastation it has become for these institutions. The transformation of the structures and organizations of the U.S. Church is essential for its reconstruction and renewal.

## The Renewal of the Spiritual Life

Many young former Catholics whom I have interviewed in Buddhist, Hindu, and Sufi spiritual communities in the United States claim that they were unable to discover an intensive spiritual experience in the Church into which they were born, and that this prompted them to leave it. Many other young people who continue to identify as Catholics share this view.

Catholics in the past have not been seen as having an impoverished spiritual tradition. Aside from the mass and the sacraments, Catholic devotional life included the rosary, an entire spectrum of pious practices, novenas, days of recollection, and retreats. Today, however, most Catholics would acknowledge that something is missing from the spiritual life put forward by the U.S. Catholic Church.

The term "spiritual life" is a tricky one. The "spiritual life" incorporates all those aspects of religious life, including prayer and what Catholics have traditionally known as "the corporal works of mercy." However, as used in the context of the comments in this chapter, the term refers to the more limited aspects of prayer and mysticism.

The mystical tradition in Catholicism reaches back to the early centuries of Christianity. Prayer and meditation have been discussed and urged by countless spiritual writers. And yet, perhaps because of the immigrant roots of U.S. Catholicism and the practical orientation of its leaders, the rich heritage of mysticism has not become part of the U.S. Catholic experience. With the surge of interest in mysticism and in an enriched life of prayer and meditation that began in the 1960s, strongly influenced by the expanded presence of Eastern religious groups in the United States, the U.S. Catholic Church found itself in the extraordinary position of not being able to convey the possibilities of this spiritual tradition to its members.

As increasing numbers of Americans of all faiths practiced transcendental meditation, chanted in Hindu ashrams, meditated in Zen Buddhist centers, and eagerly read the classics of mysticism from all religions, the U.S. Catholic Church could not tap its own spiritual roots for the spiritual enrichment of its members. One woman who asked her pastor to teach her how to read the breviary (a privately recited version of the monastic Divine Office) was told, "It's a pain in the neck for priests to do. Why do you want to do it?" A young man who suggested to his pastor that he might inaugurate the daily saying or chanting of Lauds in the morning and Vespers in the evening in the church was asked, "Who would come?" Another priest reportedly told someone who wished to discuss the mysticism of John of the Cross that, "that mystical stuff is only for the very few chosen by God."

Even the Society of Jesus, which had pioneered the movements of retreats for laypersons based upon Ignatius of Loyola's *Spiritual Exercises*, had watered down this experience to weekends of pallid moral exhortations.

Thus the heightened spiritual consciousness of the contemporary United States found no correspondingly eager Catholic Church to share its rich and diverse spiritual tradition. No parish priests inaugurated the recitation or chanting of the Divine Office in their churches. No instruction was provided on methods of meditation. No attempts were made to have time set aside for meditation in common. No sermons or other talks were given proclaiming mystical union with God to be the goal of *every* Catholic. It is no wonder that most U.S. Catholics thought—and think—that mysticism is an exotic aspect of the Church. Nor is it any wonder that those who sought such an enhanced spiritual life drifted off to Zen centers, Hindu ashrams, and Sufi communities.

There seems to be no doubt that an increasing number of

Catholics in the United States are seeking *more*, not less, in the way of spiritual experience. If the U.S. Catholic Church is unable to feed this spiritual hunger, many of them will go elsewhere. The Divine Office, that beautiful, ancient prayer, need not be relegated only to monasteries or to the daily required recitation by priests. It can become part of the common patrimony of all Catholics—both as private and as public prayer. Meditation, which even those with no religious affiliation have discovered has a beneficial, centering effect, needs to be offered to Catholics for the enhancement of their spiritual lives. Mysticism—that profound experience of union with God—should be incorporated into the spiritual experience of Catholics as part of an authentic spiritual tradition—not as an exotic or esoteric phenomenon open only to a select few. The Jesus Prayer, so similar to the Eastern mantra, could be explained to Catholics; and *authentic* Ignatian spirituality could be expounded to the thousands of retreatants who dutifully and annually experience Jesuit retreat houses.

The revival of the Catholic tradition of spirituality dovetails with an emerging sense of Catholic community—people worshiping and praying together. The most obvious centers for energizing this spiritual revival are the increasingly un-used parish complexes. Rather than preside over virtually empty structures, the pastors and curates of the thousands of parishes throughout the United States could begin to inculcate their flocks with these spiritual practices, open up their churches and parish halls to those who seek an expanded spiritual life, and bring together those who seek a community of prayer and worship in their lives.

## The Development of a Sexual Ethic and a Social Gospel

U.S. Catholicism has often devoted its energies to preaching puritanism in sexuality and has tended to ignore the social gospel. In this it was abetted in 1968 by Pope Paul VI's issuance of the anti-birth control encyclical, *Humanae Vitae*. There is no doubt that the Church's credibility as a teacher of sexual ethics plummeted following the proclamation of the pope's proscription of artificial birth control and that U.S. Catholic religious practices declined substantially in its aftermath. At the same time, while denouncing the birth control pill, the Church's leadership had virtually nothing to say about the social responsibility of Catholics.

This is not the place for an extensive treatment of these two aspects of the Church in contemporary society—its teaching on sexuality and its teaching of the social gospel—except to summarize the impoverishment of its teachings as a factor in the reconstruction of U.S. Catholicism. Many observers believe that the Church's teaching on birth control will eventually be left entirely to the discretion of the Catholic layperson and his or her confessor or spiritual advisor (as is done in the Eastern Orthodox Church). However, such a process—already increasingly a practical matter in U.S. Catholicism—will take decades before it functions smoothly, and before the memory is erased of Pope Paul's defiance both of the commission he appointed to examine the matter and of the feeling of the Catholic community at large.

A theology of sex and love could be developed out of the disaster of *Humanae Vitae*—a theology that is very much needed in the contemporary United States. Marriage and love between individuals is no longer what it was in the late Roman Empire, the Middle Ages, the Renaissance, or even the first half of the twentieth century. The economic imperatives of these earlier eras as the basis for marriage no longer function. We have a new consciousness of the enhancing synergy brought about by the love of two people in marriage. And, while one need not subscribe to the excesses of the sexual revolution of the 1960s and 1970s, we have a new consciousness about the importance of sexuality in relationships. The Church could have a great deal to say—and a great deal of guidance to give—to men and women in the United States, buffeted by the conflicts that surround the subjects of marriage, sex, and relationships in contemporary society.

The same kind of void could be filled by the development of a theology of social responsibility. Very little has been said as to why the rich young man went away sad after he had asked Jesus what he must do to gain eternal life. Jesus told him that he must keep the commandments, and the man responded that he had always kept them. Jesus said, "If you wish to be perfect, go and sell what you own and give the money to the poor ... then come, follow me." [6] Evangelical poverty traditionally has been seen as one of the criteria for monastic and other manifestations of religious life; but the Church has never developed a theology of poverty or of the common patrimony of property.

As with the complex of marriage, relationships, and sexuality, contemporary society has raised consciousness about poverty. Do affluent nations have the right to excessive consumption while millions go hungry, unclothed, and unhoused in other countries? In the face of the increasing scarcity of the planet's resources, what is the morality of continued consumption as we have known it in the United States?

The role of Jesus' teachings on poverty in the life of Christians has been the subject of examination throughout the history of Christianity—from the Acts of the Apostles to the meeting held by Pope John Paul II at Puebla, Mexico, in 1978. At no other time in history, however, has the ownership of goods been more under scrutiny; and there are many who believe that the numerous statements of Jesus on voluntary poverty present the basis for a more equitable distribution of these goods throughout the world.

There is no doubt that the United States provides an ideal environment in which to preach the social gospel; and the U.S. Catholic Church could unfold a theology of the social gospel to a country that—despite the increasing economic constraints of the past few years—combines rich resources with an idealism about sharing those resources.[7] The U.S. Catholic Church has splendid precedents for such a theology in the lives and works of Dorothy Day and Peter Maurin.

That the social gospel needs to go to the heart of the contemporary socioeconomic society is enunciated by David J. O'Brien:

> In today's world simple expressions of charity are not enough; dedication to Christian service means something more, must mean something more, than visiting the sick and the aged or cleaning up the house of a crowded family. It must mean political action, attempts to organize the poor themselves and those

who are concerned about the poor in order to obtain influence and power. The problems of American society are fundamentally structural problems and not problems of personal greed and selfishness. Problems of poverty, discrimination, poor housing and the aged are problems that must be dealt with first of all on a public level; they necessitate a fundamental reordering of the distribution of power in society. All those who feel a fundamental responsibility for their fellow man, and particularly for the oppressed and the poverty-stricken, must join together.[8]

———

What, then, is the future of U.S. Catholicism? What will the U.S. Catholic Church look like in coming years? Certain predictable marks stand out in bold relief, while other observations on the future of the U.S. Church are offered as intuitions that may or may not come to pass. The present is still too fluid to give much sense of the future.

The past and present, however, combine to tell us that U.S. Catholicism in the future will be a structural pluralism. Gone, probably forever, will be that monolithic uniformity that marked the U.S. Catholic Church prior to the Second Vatican Council. This diversity need not mean instability, however. Christianity developed distinctive liturgies and spiritualities as it spread throughout the Roman Empire, and U.S. Catholicism can follow a similar course today. Catholic charismatic communities will exist side-by-side with Catholic groups that will dedicate their lives to social apostolates and gather together each day to recite the Divine Office. Some Catholics will celebrate the liturgy in a mass that preserves as much as it can of the structured cadences of the Tridentine mass; others will gravitate toward a more intimate, more contemporary *agape*. The geographical parish will continue to exist; and new kinds of Catholic communities—reconstituted parishes, perhaps—will come into existence.

I believe the historical and institutional Catholic Church will reassert itself in the future; and the relics of the formless "underground Church" that continue to exist will evaporate. This does not mean that there will cease to be what I call the "cultural Catholic"—the person who, for whatever reason, chooses to look upon himself or herself as a Catholic without committing to those practices that have traditionally been the prescribed duties of Catholics. Such "cultural Catholics" will probably be a larger component of U.S. Catholicism than they have been in the past. But the attempts of those whom James Hitchcock calls "radical Catholics" [9] to form cells of Catholics, eschewing authority in the Church and based more or less outside the structures of the institutional Church are destined for failure—and the "underground Church" is doomed to extinction.

This does not mean that experimentation with ideas and forms will not continue. Catholics within the institutional structure will reconcile themselves to this continuing experimentation and to the developing plurality of structures related in various ways to the central hierarchy. Freedom and movement, at the expense of order and clarity, will continue to be features of U.S. Catholicism—although without the divisive, disintegrating results of the decade following the Second Vatican Council. O'Brien gives his vision of this conjunction between freedom and order:

> . . . The bishops should regard the present ferment as an opportunity rather than a threat, should look for potential rather than search out dangers. The old church may well have sinned on the side of order, authority, clarity of doctrine and of structure; the new church might compensate by moving in the opposite direction. No institution likes to pay the price of freedom: inefficiency, lack of respect for guidelines and formal authority, frequent aberrations and even irrationality. But the lesson of history is clear: the Catholic church preserved itself, its power and influence, at the cost of much of its dynamism and messianic drive. More than other institutions, the church must fear not deviation but rigidity, not rebellious attempts to reach the reality behind itself but its own natural tendency to identify itself with that reality." [10]

It seems realistic—although by no means a certainty—to assume that new forms of leadership will emerge in U.S. Catholicism. The Catholic layperson, heretofore relegated to a role that can best be described by the aphorism, "pray, pay, and keep quiet," will be called upon more and more to administer the Church. Even a surge of vocations to the priesthood and religious life in future years will not provide the numbers necessary to administer every aspect of the Church, as was true in the past, and the sacramental role of the priest will be emphasized through sheer necessity. Lay deacons, ordained for specific ministerial roles, will expand the services of the Church.

The spiritual life of the Church will reflect the pluralism described above. While traditional devotions—the Rosary, nocturnal adoration, etc.—will probably experience a renaissance, I also believe that the mystical tradition, influenced by Orthodox and Far Eastern spirituality, will be of great moment in the U.S. Catholicism of the future.

This observation about the future of the spiritual diversity in U.S. Catholicism is based upon the intense interest in the spiritual life and in mysticism now so prevalent in the United States. Some of this interest, of course, merely reflects an intellectual search for the esoteric. But many people today believe personal union with God to be equally, if not more important than intellectual acceptance of religious precepts. That external influences should spark the U.S. Catholic Church to reanimate and to rediscover its own rich spiritual tradition is but another example of how the Church has become increasingly assimilated into the cultural *ethos* of the United States.

We see at this time the beginnings of a resurgence of spirituality in such movements as the houses of prayer, the rise in centering prayer being taught to Catholics, meditation becoming an increasing part of the spiritual life of Catholics, and the current popularity of new editions of Catholic spiritual classics and mystical treatises such as *The Cloud of Unknowing,* and the works of Teresa of Avila and John of the Cross.

Finally, the U.S. Catholic Church of the future will probably discover and implement new forms of community life—a new monasticism, if you will. The need for this has been discussed above; and we have already seen Catholic charismatic communities come into being. Although the collective life is not new to Catholicism nor to the United States, social and economic forces today give it a new imperative. The experience of other religious groups (e.g., Buddhist and Hindu spiritual communities, the Holy Order of MANS) will help to lead the way. Characteristics of such Catholic spiritual communities will include, I believe, a new interpretation of traditional vows, mixed communities of men and women, communities of families, and communities of those who will continue to work at outside jobs while pursuing an apostolate in common.

David O'Brien, writing in the early 1970s amidst the strife and institutional disintegration of U.S. Catholicism, and perhaps with too much faith in a political model, uttered a vision of the Church that he intuited would be based on the phenomenon of the collective. Such a collective/ecclesiastical community, O'Brien maintains, would have the common affirmation of Jesus Christ and would find its meaning not in itself but in the goal it seeks. He writes:

> Thus, the collective may be for some the new form of the church, providing a structure within which communities of men and women join together for worship, proclamation, fellowship and service. Acknowledging their unity with other Christian communities and with other groups working for the advent of God's Kingdom, the collective-church accepts the tension and ambiguity of the historical situation, poised on the threshold between past and future, between the here and now world of power and promise and the coming Kingdom of freedom and righteousness, and it acknowledges both with utmost seriousness.[11]

O'Brien's thesis is an interesting portrayal of the Church seen as a visible presence of the response to the Gospel. And, indeed, the continuing revolutionary dynamic of the Gospel message and the ever-present role of the Incarnation in history demands a radical *metanoia*—a conversion of "the people of God" to the possibility of redemption implied in Jesus Christ's birth, death, and resurrection.

For the Church, there can be no compromise, no attempt to return to the "good old days" of pre-Vatican II, no sloth in galvanizing the spiritual energies of its members. The preaching and acceptance of the "good news" means that one's life is altered, transformed, charged with the fact that God sent His Only Begotten Son to take on flesh and to live and die for mankind.

The decade of the 1980s will be a crucial one for the U.S. Catholic Church. Its ability to reach out to all with Christ's message will determine whether, in the far-distant future, historians will be able to look back upon this period in the life of the Church and dub it a "second spring."

### Notes

Full publication information for works cited here can be found in the Bibliography.

## Chapter 1

1  So great, in fact, that I have never in my life masturbated. The fear of God's punishment in the afterlife and of some dread mental or physical disease has been replaced by other considerations on this subject, however—considerations that revolve around the solitariness of masturbation as a sexual act.

## Chapter 2

1  Greeley, *The Catholic Experience*, p. 19.

2  McAvoy, *A History of the Catholic Church in the United States*, p. 242.

3  Greeley, *The Catholic Experience*, p. 150.

4  Ibid., p. 151.

5  Most agree that statistics on Catholics, reported in the *Official Catholic Directory*, are unreliable: that the figures should be substantially higher than those reported. These discrepancies arise from pastors sending in the same figures year after year and from no accurate census being taken.

6  This distinctive Catholic experience in the United States as part of the immigrant experience can still be seen among more recent immigrants: Mexican parishes in Los Angeles, for example, with a widespread and lively devotion to Our Lady of Guadalupe, or Filipino parishes in San Francisco with altars to Santo Nino de Cebu.

## Chapter 3

1  An excellent account of *Commonweal* and its impact on Catholicism in the United States is contained in Rodger Van Allen's *The Commonweal and American Catholicism*.

2  Greeley, *The Catholic Experience*, p. 247. Greeley's chapter, "The Chicago Experience" (pp. 247–274) is an outstanding account of the importance of the developments in Chicago and the Midwest in the 1930s and 1940s.

3  McAvoy, *A History of the Catholic Church in the United States*, p. 445.

4  The central essay in this controversy was that of Monsignor John Tracy Ellis, "American Catholics and the Intellectual Life" (Chicago, 1956). The paper was first given in St. Louis on May 14, 1955, and then published in *Thought* (1955), XII, 351–388.

5  Wills, *Bare Ruined Choirs*, p. 39.

6  *Cf.*, Garry Wills, "A Farewell (Quite Fond) to the Catholic Liberal," *The Critic* 29:3 (January–February, 1971), pp. 14–22; and George Devine, *Liturgical Renewal*, p. 39 (footnote no. 1).

7  Wills, *Bare Ruined Choirs*, pp. 39–40.

8  Ibid., pp. 41–42.

9  Ibid., p. 47.

10  Ibid., p. 58.

11  The publication which was most involved in defining the literary tastes of Catholic liberals at this time was *Renascence*—the journal of the Catholic Renascence Society.

12  An encyclical is a "circulating letter" (in Latin *literae encyclicae*). Used originally by bishops in the early Church (they seem to have begun in the fourth century), encyclicals were sent from bishop to bishop to gather signatures against heretical movements. The modern usage of the encyclical dates back to the eighteenth century. It then became a less formal method for papal communication. The Pope could—and does—use the encyclical to celebrate an event or anniversary, restore a devotion, praise a religious order, to warn of evil trends or practices, encourage worthy projects, to explain his action (as when Pius IX issued *Quanta Cura* to justify his issuance of *The Syllabus of Errors*), and to state Catholic principles on some matter. An encyclical is known by the first two Latin words of the title of the document.

13  This phenomenon—like so many other aspects of Catholicism—has yet to be written about. In the light of a Bible fundamentalism which is now popular with a growing segment of the U.S. Catholic Church, a study of this movement would be most illuminating.

14  Actually, it merged into *U.S. Catholic*.

## Chapter 4

1  The text of Pope John XXIII's address at the solemn opening of the Vatican Council II, October 11, 1962, is found as Appendix I in Xavier Rynne's *Letters From Vatican City*, pp. 262–272.

2  This refers to the form of the mass of the Latin—or Western—rite, which was established by the Council of Trent in the sixteenth century. The liturgical uniformity sparked by this reform succeeded in creating a uniform Latin rite mass for four centuries.

3  Rynne tells an amusing story about the reaction of an Italian archbishop after listening to Cardinal Spellman and Cardinal McIntyre vigorously defend the retention of Latin in the mass and then state that priests be allowed to read their breviaries in English. "Ah! *Questi Americani!*" he has him say, "Now they want the priest to pray in English, and the people to pray in Latin" (Rynne, *Letters From Vatican City*, p. 125).

4  Rynne, *The Fourth Session*, p. 184.

5  *Dogmatic Constitution on the Church*, Chapter II, Section 9, in Rynne, *The Third Session*, p. 304.

6  Ibid., *Dogmatic Constitution on the Church*, Chapter II, Section 16, p. 309.

7  Ibid., *Decree on Ecumenism*, Chapter I, Section 3, p. 353.

8  Ibid., *Decree on Ecumenism*, Chapter I, Section 4, pp. 354–355.

9  *Declaration on the Relation of the Church to Non-Christian Religions*, Section 2, in Rynne, *The Fourth Session*, p. 334.

10  Ibid., *Declaration on Religious Freedom*, Section 1, p. 349.

11  Ibid., *Declaration on Religious Freedom*, Section 2, p. 350.

12  Ibid., pp. 253–254.

13  My objection to Greeley's conclusion, based on his sociological data, is based on my question: *Humanae Vitae* was merely a restatement of traditional (at least during the twentieth century) Catholic teaching; why was this teaching accepted, if not always followed, previous to the issuance of *Humanae Vitae?*

14  Hitchcock's two books on contemporary Catholicism are *The Decline and Fall of Radical Catholicism* and *The Church and the Modern World.*

## *Chapter 5*

1  For a brilliantly written account of the move of the Jesuit theologate from Woodstock, Maryland, to New York City and its existence there (before being closed), see Garry Wills' *Bare Ruined Choirs,* pp. 191–229.

2  Greeley, et al., *Catholic Schools in a Declining Church,* p. 106.

3  Ibid., pp. 106–107.

4  Ibid., p. 107.

5  Ibid., p. 108.

6  Several authors have discussed this subject. Garry Wills, in *Bare Ruined Choirs,* is perhaps most incisive in his critique of Catholic absorption with the secular during this period.

7  *National Catholic Reporter* (hereinafter referred to as *NCR*), December 23, 1964, pp. 1 and 5.

8  *NCR,* June 23, 1965, pp. 1 and 10.

9  *NCR,* July 7, 1965, pp. 1 and 10.

10  *NCR,* July 7, 1965, p. 10.

11  *NCR,* April 4, 1965, p. 1.

12  *NCR,* December 1, 1965, p. 1.

13  *NCR,* December 22, 1965, p. 3.

14  *NCR,* March 30, 1966, p. 1.

15  *NCR,* June 29, 1966, p. 3.

16  Andrew Greeley discusses the question of Catholic schools in many of his books—most notably *Catholic Schools in a Declining Church,* of which he is a co-author. Among his contentions, based upon his sociological surveys, are that most of the criticisms leveled against Catholic schools are unfounded; that, despite rising costs, most parents would have been willing to contribute more money to their upkeep; and that the near-dismantlement of the Catholic school system was the result of a failure of nerve and will on the part of bishops and priests.

17  *NCR,* September 9, 1966, p. 11.

18  *NCR,* January 4, 1967.

19  For an account of Sister Jacqueline Grennan's career and role in U.S. Catholicism, see Wills, *Bare Ruined Choirs,* pp. 118–138.

20  *NCR,* November 16, 1967, p. 3.

21  *NCR,* April 26, 1967, pp. 1 and 5.

22  *NCR,* November 1, 1967, p. 1.

23  *NCR,* November 15, 1967, p. 1.

24  *NCR,* December 15, 1967, pp. 1 and 6.

25  *NCR*, March 6, 1968, p. 10.

26  *NCR*, May 29, 1968, p. 5.

27  *NCR*, June 16, 1968, p. 5.

28  *NCR*, July 17, 1968, pp. 1 and 7.

29  *NCR*, August 7, 1968, p. 1.

30  *NCR*, July 24, 1968, pp. 1 and 2.

31  *NCR*, November 27, 1968, p. 1.

32  *NCR*, October 30, 1968, pp. 1 and 10.

33  *NCR*, November 6, 1968, pp. 3 and 12.

34  *NCR*, October 23, 1968, p. 3.

35  *NCR*, November 20, 1968, p. 7.

36  *NCR*, November 20, 1968, p. 2.

37  *NCR*, May 14, 1969, pp. 1 and 5.

38  *NCR*, December 11, 1968, p. 4.

39  *NCR*, April 2, 1969, pp. 1 and 2.

40  *NCR*, June 4, 1969, pp. 1 and 9.

41  *NCR*, September 3, 1969, pp. 1 and 6.

42  *NCR*, December 3, 1969, p. 8.

43  *NCR*, December 3, 1969, p. 5.

44  *NCR*, November 27, 1970, p. 3.

45  *NCR*, February 5, 1971, p. 1.

46  *NCR*, January 21, 1972, p. 20.

47  *NCR*, November 3, 1972, pp. 1 and 5.

48  *NCR*, March 9, 1972, p. 18.

49  *NCR*, November 16, 1973, p. 1.

50  *NCR*, November 16, 1973, p. 17.

51  *NCR*, February 8, 1974, p. 7.

52  *NCR*, December 4, 1970, p. 3.

53  *NCR*, February 19, 1971, pp. 1 and 16.

54  *NCR*, December 4, 1970, p. 7.

55  *NCR*, November 23, 1973, p. 7.

56  *NCR*, November 1, 1974, p. 2.

57  Greeley, et al., *Catholic Schools in a Declining Church*, p. 9.

58  Ibid., p. 9.

59  Ibid., pp. 29–30.

60  Ibid., p. 32.

61  Ibid., p. 32.

62  *NCR*, April 26, 1974, p. 1.

63  *NCR*, July 10, 1970, p. 12.

64  Wills, *Bare Ruined Choirs*, pp. 97–117; Eppstein, *Has the Catholic Church Gone Mad?*, pp. 109–116.

65  Eppstein, *Has the Catholic Church Gone Mad?*, pp. 115–116.

## Chapter 6

1  Expressions such as "progressive" (or "liberal") and "conservative" (or "traditionalist") are inadequate but unavoidable. They do not, in this context, have the same meaning as the terms usually do in political parlance. With regard to liturgical matters, I define a "progressive" as one who wishes to see maximum flexibility and radical change in the liturgy and a "conservative" as one who wishes a return to some sort of variation—certainly from an aesthetic point of view—of the Tridentine mass.

2  Devine, *American Catholicism: Where Do We Go from Here?*, pp. 43–44.

3  Ibid., p. 44.

4  Ibid., p. 46.

5  Devine, *Liturgical Renewal: An Agonizing Reappraisal*, pp. 113–114.

6  Greeley, *Come Blow Your Mind with Me*, pp. 80–81.

7  The form of mass which was finalized at the Council of Trent in the mid-sixteenth century.

8  Eppstein, *Has the Catholic Church Gone Mad?*, pp. 45–76.

9  Wills, *Bare Ruined Choirs*, p. 65.

10  Hitchcock, *The Decline and Fall of Radical Catholicism*, p. 213.

11  A prime example of this is the Ave Maria Chapel at Old Westbury, Long Island, operated by Father Gommar De Pauw and his Catholic Traditionalist Movement.

12  Devine, *Liturgical Renewal: An Agonizing Reappraisal*, p. 76.

13  Hitchcock, *The Decline and Fall of Radical Catholicism*, p. 212.

14  Devine, *American Catholicism: Where Do We Go from Here?*, p. 53.

15  The antiphon in English is as follows: May the angels lead thee into paradise: may the martyrs receive thee at thy coming, and lead thee into the holy city of Jerusalem. May the choir of angels receive thee, and mayest thou have eternal rest with Lazarus, who once was poor.

## Chapter 7

1  The story of the beginning of the Catholic charismatic movement is told in the first chapter of *Catholic Pentecostals* by Kevin and Dorothy Ranaghan.

2  Pentecostalism is usually referred to in its Catholic manifestations as "the charismatic movement." Both words—"Pentecostal" and "charismatic"—mean essentially the same thing, and can be used interchangeably.

3  In an article entitled, "Glossolalia: 'It's Rooted in Emotional Disturbance,' " in the *National Catholic Reporter*, October 2, 1970, p. 17.

4  McNamara, *Mystical Passion*, p. 72.

5  Quoted in O'Connor, *The Pentecostal Movement in the Catholic Church*, p. 21. The full report is given in an appendix to the book, pp. 291–293.

6  I have taken this account from O'Connor, *The Pentecostal Movement in the Catholic Church*, p. 22.

7  Acts of the Apostles, 2, 1–4.

8  1 Corinthians, 12, 8–10.

9 Gelpi, *Pentecostalism: A Theological Viewpoint*, p. 125.

10 My purpose is not to pass judgment on the nature of the charismatic gifts. There are a number of excellent accounts that attempt to examine their qualities. One of the best of these, dealing with speaking in tongues, is Morton Kelsey's *Tongue Speaking: An Experiment in Spiritual Experience* (New York: Doubleday, 1968).

11 This historical response has been true of all three major branches of Christianity: Catholic, Protestant, and Orthodox. An example within Catholicism is the condemnation and uprooting of the Waldenses and Cathari during the Middle Ages, and the transformation and assimilation of the Franciscans.

12 Condemnation of the Montanists (as well as of other similar groups throughout the history of the Church) has during recent years been the subject of revised thinking. Some scholars believe that officials in the Church overreacted to what they considered the doctrinal and spiritual dangers of Montanism.

13 A priest active in the charismatic movement whom I interviewed stated that another problem with such rigid leadership is that it tended to exclude women from positions of responsibility and leadership.

14 Fichter, *The Catholic Cult of the Paraclete*, pp. 37–38.

15 Ibid., p. 137.

16 Ibid., p. 131.

## Chapter 8

1 O'Brien, *The Renewal of American Catholicism*, p. xiii.

2 Hitchcock, *Catholicism and Modernity*, p. 231.

3 Novak, *All the Catholic People*, p. 63.

4 I could multiply examples of "dead" parishes *ad infinitum*. If readers think I am over-generalizing in this matter, visit a random selection of parish churches on a Sunday.

5 I have covered this matter of the burgeoning of spiritual communities in the United States in my book, *Living Together Alone: The New American Monasticism* (Harper & Row, Inc., 1979).

6 Matthew, 19, 16–22.

7 For further consideration of the social gospel and the possibilities for contemporary Catholics in what has come to be called "simple living," Adam Finnerty's *No More Plastic Jesus: Global Justice and Christian Lifestyle* provides an excellent starting point.

8 O'Brien, *The Renewal of American Catholicism*, p. 136.

9 Hitchcock's use of the word "radical" in his book *The Decline and Fall of Radical Catholicism* leaves something to be desired. The ambiguity of the word arises from the fact that he uses it to embrace every Catholic on the so-called "left"— from liberal reformers to those who would dismantle the historical, institutional Church for some vague structureless "body of believers."

10 O'Brien, *The Renewal of American Catholicism*, p. 262.

11 Ibid., pp. 274–275.

## Bibliography

### Periodicals

The files of the following periodicals were used extensively: *The Critic, Jubilee, National Catholic Reporter, Worship.*

### Books

Abbott, Walter M., S.J., editor. *The Documents of Vatican II.* New York: Herder and Herder/Association Press, 1966.

Bausch, William L. *Renewal and the Middle Catholic.* Notre Dame, Indiana: Fides Publishers, 1971.

Berger, Peter. *A Rumor of Angels.* Garden City, New York: Doubleday and Company, 1969.

Berger, Peter and Richard Neuhaus, editors. *Against the World, For the World.* New York: Seabury Press, 1976.

Berkouwer, G. C. *The Second Vatican Council and the New Catholicism.* Translated by Lewis B. Smedes. Grand Rapids, Michigan: William B. Eerdmans Publishing Company, 1965.

Bloesch, Donald C. *The Reform of the Church.* Grand Rapids, Michigan: William B. Eerdmans Publishing Company, 1970.

Bouyer, Louis C. *The Decomposition of Catholicism.* Translated with a forward by Charles Underhill Quinn. Chicago: Franciscan Herald Press, 1969.

Callahan, Daniel. *The Mind of the Catholic Layman.* New York: Scribner's, 1963.

Callahan, Daniel. *The New Church: Essays in Catholic Reform.* New York: Scribner's, 1966.

Crowe, Frederick E., S.J. *A Time of Change: Guidelines for the Perplexed Catholic.* Milwaukee: The Bruce Publishing Co., 1968.

Devine, George. *American Catholicism: Where Do We Go From Here?* Englewood Cliffs, New Jersey: Prentice-Hall, Inc., 1975.

Devine, George. *Liturgical Renewal: An Agonizing Reappraisal.* New York: Alba House, 1973.

Devine, George. *Transformation in Christ.* New York: Alba House, 1972.

Dulles, Avery, S.J. *The Resilient Church: The Necessity and Limits of Adaptation,* Garden City, New York: Doubleday & Company, Inc., 1977.

Ellis, John Tracy. *American Catholicism.* Chicago: The University of Chicago Press, 1969. Second edition, revised.

Eppstein, John. *Has the Catholic Church Gone Mad?* London: Tom Stacey Limited, 1971.

Evely, Louis. *If the Church Is to Survive . . .* Translated by J.F. Bernard. Garden City, New York: Doubleday & Company, Inc., 1972.

Fichter, Joseph H. *The Catholic Cult of the Paraclete.* New York: Sheed and Ward, Inc., 1975.

Finnerty, Adam. *No More Plastic Jesus: Global Justice and Christian Lifestyle.* Maryknoll, New York: Orbis Books, 1977.

Gelpi, Donald. *Pentecostalism: A Theological Viewpoint*. New York: Paulist Press, 1971.

Gilkey, Langdon. *Catholicism Confronts Modernity: A Protestant View*. New York: Seabury Press, 1975.

Gleason, Philip, editor. *Contemporary Catholicism in the U.S.* Notre Dame, Indiana: Notre Dame Press, 1969.

Greeley, Andrew M. *The American Catholic—A Social Portrait*. New York: Basic Books, Inc., 1977.

Greeley, Andrew M. *The Catholic Experience*. Garden City, New York: Doubleday & Co., 1967.

Greeley, Andrew M. *Come Blow Your Mind with Me*. Garden City, New York: Doubleday & Co., Inc., 1971.

Greeley, Andrew M. *The Communal Catholic*. New York: Seabury Press, 1976.

Greeley, Andrew M. *Crisis in the Church*. Chicago: The Thomas More Press, 1979.

Greeley, Andrew M. *The Hesitant Pilgrim*. New York: Sheed & Ward, Inc., 1966.

Greeley, Andrew M., William C. McCready, and Kathleen McCourt. *Catholic Schools in a Declining Church*. Kansas City: Sheed & Ward, Inc., 1976.

Hebblethwaite, Peter. *The Runaway Church: Post-Conciliar Growth or Decline*. New York: The Seabury Press, 1975.

Hitchcock, James. *Catholicism and Modernity*. New York: The Seabury Press, 1979.

Hitchcock, James. *The Decline and Fall of Radical Catholicism*. New York: Herder and Herder, 1971.

Hitchcock, James. *On the Present Position of Catholics in America*. New York: The National Committee of Catholic Laymen, 1978.

Hitchcock, James. *The Recovery of the Sacred*. New York: Seabury Press, 1974.

Kaiser, Robert. *Pope, Council and World: The Story of Vatican II*. New York: Macmillan & Co., 1963.

Kotre, John N. *The Best of Times, The Worst of Times: Andrew Greeley and American Catholicism, 1950-1975*. Chicago: Nelson-Hall Company, 1978.

McAvoy, Thomas T. *A History of the Catholic Church in the United States*. Notre Dame, Indiana: University of Notre Dame Press, 1969.

McBrien, Richard P. *The Remaking of the Church: An Agenda for Reform*. New York: Harper & Row, Inc., 1973.

McKenzie, John L. *The Roman Catholic Church*. New York: Holt, Rinehart & Winston, 1969.

McNamara, William. *Mystical Passion*. New York: Paulist Press, 1977.

Maynard, Theodore. *The Story of American Catholicism*. New York: The Macmillan Company, 1941.

National Opinion Research Center. *The Catholic Priest in the United States: Sociological Investigations*. Washington, D.C.: United States Catholic Conference, 1972.

Novak, Michael. *All the Catholic People: Where Did All the Spirit Go?* New York: Herder and Herder, 1971.

Novak, Michael. *The Open Church*. New York: Macmillan & Co., 1964.

O'Brien, David J. *The Renewal of American Catholicism*. New York: Oxford University Press, 1972.

O'Connor, Edward D. *The Pentecostal Movement in the Catholic Church.* Notre Dame, Indiana: Ave Maria Press, 1971.

O'Connor, Edward D., editor. *Perspectives on Charismatic Renewal.* Notre Dame, Indiana: University of Notre Dame Press, 1975.

O'Dea, Thomas F. *The Catholic Crisis.* Boston: Beacon Press, 1968.

Rahner, Karl. *The Shape of the Church to Come.* Translated by Edward Quinn. New York: The Seabury Press, 1974.

Ranaghan, Kevin and Dorothy Ranaghan. *Catholic Pentecostals.* New York: Paulist Press, 1969.

Roche, Douglas. *The Catholic Revolution.* New York: D. McKay Co., 1968.

Roszak, Theodore. *Person/Planet.* Garden City, New York: Anchor Books/Doubleday & Co., 1978.

Ruether, Rosemary. *The Church Against Itself.* New York: Herder and Herder, 1967.

Ruffolo, Marina E., general editor. *The Dynamic Voice of Vatican II.* Boston: St. Paul Editions, 1977.

Rynne, Xavier. *The Fourth Session.* New York: Farrar, Straus and Giroux, 1966.

Rynne, Xavier. *Letters from Vatican City.* New York: Farrar, Straus & Company, 1963.

Rynne, Xavier. *The Second Session.* New York: Farrar, Straus & Company, 1964.

Rynne, Xavier. *The Third Session.* New York: Farrar, Straus & Giroux, 1965.

Thorman, Donald J. *American Catholics Face the Future.* Wilkes-Barre, Pennsylvania: Dimension Books, 1968.

Thorman, Donald J. *Power to the People of God.* Paramus, New Jersey: Paulist Press, 1970.

Van Allan, Rodger. *The Commonweal and American Catholicism.* Philadelphia: Fortress Press, 1974.

Ward, Leo R. *Contemporary Life, U.S.A.* St. Louis: B. Herder Book Co., 1959.

Westow, Theodore. *Introducing Contemporary Catholicism.* Philadelphia: The Westminster Press, 1967.

Wills, Garry. *Bare Ruined Choirs.* Garden City, New York: Doubleday & Company, Inc., 1972.

Yzermans, Vincent A., editor. *American Participation in the Second Vatican Council.* New York: Sheed and Ward, 1967.